ALEXANDER THE GREAT

Conqueror of the Ancient World

Tom McGowen

Enslow Publishers, Inc.

40 Industrial Road   PO Box 38
Box 398   Aldershot
Berkeley Heights, NJ 07922   Hants GU12 6BP
USA   UK

http://www.enslow.com

This book is dedicated to
Lance Corporal Ryan Deady, USMC
Semper Fi, Mac

Library of Congress Cataloging-in-Publication Data

McGowen, Tom.
    Alexander the Great : conqueror of the ancient world / Tom McGowen.
        p. cm. — (Rulers of the ancient world)
    Includes bibliographical references and index.
    ISBN 0-7660-2560-8
    1. Alexander, the Great, 356–323 B.C.—Juvenile literature. 2. Greece—History—
Macedonian Expansion, 359–323 B.C.—Juvenile literature. 3. Generals—Greece—
Biography—Juvenile literature. 4. Greece—Kings and rulers—Biography—Juvenile
literature. I. Title. II. Series.
DF234.M29 2006
938'.07'092—dc22

                                                        2005022598

Printed in the United States of America

10 9 8 7 6 5 4 3 2 1

To Our Readers:
We have done our best to make sure that all Internet addresses in this book were active and
appropriate when we went to press. However, the author and publisher have no control over and
assume no liability for the material available on those Internet sites or on other Web sites they may
link to. Any comments or suggestions can be sent by e-mail to comments@enslow.com or to the
address on the back cover.

Illustration Credits: © The British Museum/HIP/The Image Works, p. 143; Clipart.com, pp. 14, 18,
20, 21, 31, 48, 78, 84, 103; © Corel Corporation, p. 110; Enslow Publishers, Inc., pp. 12, 90–91; J. G.
Heck, ed., *Heck's Pictorial Archive of Military Science, Georgraphy, and History*, published by Dover
Publications, Inc., in 1994, design at the top of pp. 5, 16, 26, 35, 43, 53, 62, 74, 86, 96, 105, 115, 123,
133 and images on pp. 94, 127, 144; Photos.com, p. 33; Reproduced from the Collections of the
Library of Congress, pp. 6, 46; ©Topham/The Image Works, p. 1.

Subhead Illustrations: J. G. Heck, ed., *Heck's Pictorial Archive of Military Science, Georgraphy, and
History,* published by Dover Publications, Inc., in 1994.

Cover Illustration: © Topham/The Image Works

CONTENTS

KING, GENERAL, LEGEND

The city of Multan was under attack!

It was a very old city in what is now the nation of India. A high, thick brick wall stood around it. A foreign army swarmed outside the wall, setting up ladders against it. Soldiers defending the city, up on top of the wall, looked down with anxious eyes. They knew it would not be long before they would be confronted face-to-face by enemy soldiers.

Suddenly, one foreigner did come over the wall, leaping down to engage a group of Multan's soldiers. The soldiers froze, staring at him in awe and astonishment. Clearly, this was no ordinary soldier facing them. His armor and helmet gave off the glitter of polished gold, and a fan of white plumes sprouted from the crest of his helmet. They knew this could only be one man. They had been hearing of him for many months. He was the commander of the army attacking their city, and no

Alexander the Great

city he had ever attacked had been able to withstand him. He had commanded scores of battles, and won every one of them. He had conquered the greatest empire that had ever existed in the western world, and now he was conquering the kingdoms in the East. It was said that he was a god. The soldiers knew they were looking at Alexander, King of Macedonia.

Alexander's soldiers came over the wall behind him. The soldiers of Multan rushed forward. A hacking, thrusting fight began, men stabbing with spears and slicing with swords. Each man glared into his opponent's eyes, intent on killing him face-to-face.

A Brush With Death

Suddenly, an arrow struck King Alexander in the chest. He staggered backward and dropped to his knees. With shouts of fury, his soldiers clustered about him, protecting him with their shields. More of his soldiers poured over the wall and rushed past, cutting down the Multan soldiers. In another part of the city, the rest of Alexander's army swarmed in through a gate that had been smashed open.

Alexander was carried down to his tent outside the city. His doctor cut the shaft of the arrow, then pulled the arrowhead out of his body. This made the wound bigger, and blood spurted furiously. Within the city, the shouts of thousands of men and the screams of thousands of women and children created a steady shrieking roar. A rumor that Alexander was dead had reached his army, and his men butchered nearly everyone in the city in revenge.

Alexander's wound was a very serious one. The arrow had pierced his lung, but he did not die. This man was incredibly strong and healthy, and he survived. Within seven days, he was walking and waving weakly to his soldiers. They erupted with cheers. As long as this man lived, they believed they could never be defeated.

A LEGENDARY CONQUEROR

The man who became known as Alexander the Great was born more than two thousand years ago, in July of 356 B.C.[1] He was a prince, born into the royal family of Macedonia, a small kingdom in southeast Europe. When he grew up, he changed the world of his time. He is remembered to the present day as one of the greatest leaders in world history.

Many of the stories that tell of Alexander's deeds seem like legends—tales of a man who is almost superhuman. He was one of the greatest generals. He did not lose a single battle of the many he fought. He wound up conquering most of the known world of his time. He was apparently incredibly brave, nearly always going into battle at the head of his troops. And this was head-to-head fighting with spears and swords. He was wounded in battle eight times, twice very seriously.[2]

Most of what we know for sure about Alexander comes from people who lived long after he did. Some people that knew him when he was alive actually wrote about him. Two of those men were Ptolemy and

Aristobulus, officers in Alexander's army who knew him well. They both wrote records of Alexander's battles, but no copies of those records exist today.

However, a man known as Arrian, who lived some four hundred years after Ptolemy and Aristobulus, had copies of their books and wrote a history of Alexander based on them. Much of what we know about Alexander comes from Arrian.

LOST FACTS, MANY QUESTIONS

A number of writers and historians who lived long after Alexander's time wrote about him, using material that came from people who had known him. But these histories sometimes disagree about things Alexander did and why he did them.

FANTASTIC TALES OF ALEXANDER

Many ancient stories about Alexander come from Asia. Some of them are wildly fantastic. One tells of a time when Alexander explored the sky, carried there on a platform pulled by four griffins (winged lions). Another tells of how Alexander explored the bottom of the sea inside a huge air-filled glass bottle lowered from a ship.

These imaginary stories show that Alexander was regarded with awe by people of ancient times, as a person capable of doing incredible things. They may also show that Alexander was interested in exploring and in studying Greek philosophy, which was a mystery to the people of Asia.

Thus, many things about Alexander are unknown. We do not even know for certain what he looked like. Paintings and statues were made of him while he was alive, but none of them are known to exist today. However, copies were made of some of the original paintings and statues by artists who lived later, and they give us an idea of what he probably looked like. The artists generally made him look quite handsome, and several people who wrote about him say that he was. Some writers say he had reddish-brown hair and blue eyes, while others say he was golden-haired. A Roman mosaic based on a painting from Alexander's time shows him as brown-haired and brown-eyed. One ancient writer said he was tall; another said he was rather short and stocky. Unlike most men of his time, he did not wear a beard. It was said that he believed a beard made too good a handle for an enemy to grab![3]

ALEXANDER'S WORLD

At the time of Alexander's birth, Europe was very different from what it is now. The large nations of France, Germany, Italy, and Russia did not yet exist. Instead, there were many little kingdoms and regions inhabited by groups of tribes. Wars were frequent, as one kingdom or tribe tried to seize land from another. It was important for people to have as much land as possible for hunting and for growing crops and raising animals to feed themselves.

Alexander was born in Macedonia in southeastern Europe. It was a land of mountains, valleys, and a broad plain, covering parts of what are now the nations of Serbia, Bulgaria, and Greece. Most of the Macedonian people lived in small villages. A single large city, named Pella, was home to the king's palace. To the north and west of Macedonia was a mountainous region called Illyria that is now Albania. To the east was another mountainous area called Thrace, covering what is now part of Bulgaria and the European part of Turkey. These two regions were occupied by a number of tribes. South of Macedonia were the lands known as Hellas, which is now the nation of Greece.

Greece was one of the most important parts of Europe then, but it was not a country. The Greeks had created a number of city-states. A city-state consisted of a city or large town, with a number of little villages scattered around it, and a large area of farmland surrounding everything. The city-states were all independent of one another. The most important, because of their wealth and power, were Athens, in the region called Attica; Sparta, in Laconia; and Thebes, in Boeotia. There were a large number of smaller ones as well. Most of the people of a city-state believed they were all descended from the same ancestors, and thought of themselves much as if they were one big family. Even though the people of every city-state spoke Greek, and all considered themselves Hellenes (people of Hellas), they generally felt their own city-state was best and often looked down on others. City-states even went to war with one another.

THE RISE OF MACEDONIA

Macedonia, 359 B.C.   342 B.C.   338 B.C.

Under Alexander the Great's father, Philip II, Macedonia would conquer many nearby lands. However, Alexander would soon have to finish the job his father started.

DEMOCRACY AND SLAVERY

Unlike some regions nearby, the Greek city-states were not ruled by kings. Many were ruled by a group of the city's wealthiest men. Some were ruled by the wealthiest family. Some of them had the kind of government in which those who control the government and make the laws are chosen by votes of the people.

Every free male citizen of city-states such as Athens and Thebes had the right to vote and to serve on the council that made the city-state's laws. All free men were regarded as equal under the law.

Democracy, this idea of having a government that is run by the people who live under it, was a Greek invention. The name comes from two Greek words that mean "people rule."

The democracy of ancient Greece was not much like the democracy of a nation such as the United States today. Women were not permitted to vote. Slavery was a common custom, with most wealthy Hellenes owning a number of slaves. In the democracies, slaves were not allowed to vote. Most slaves were people who had been taken prisoner when their city was captured in a war; some were unwanted abandoned children who were made slaves; some were criminals who were made slaves as punishment; and some were people who simply could not make a living on their own and accepted slavery in order to stay alive. Slaves in Greek society were usually not slaves for life and could buy their way out of slavery.

A DANGEROUS ENEMY

Along with democratic government, Greeks were very accomplished in the fields of art, literature, and science. Greeks were intensely proud of their way of life, and in general, they looked down on the people of the lands around them as barbarians. Most of those lands, including Macedonia, were tiny kingdoms, but to the east of Greece, across a narrow strip of seawater called the Hellespont (now called the Dardanelles), was the mighty empire of Persia.

Persia was made up of what are now parts of Iran and Afghanistan. Some twenty-five hundred years ago, it began conquering the lands around it in the Middle East. By the time of Alexander's birth, Persia was enormous, stretching more than three thousand miles across what

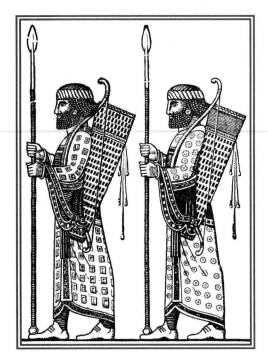

are now the countries of Pakistan, Afghanistan, Iran, Turkey, Syria, Jordan, Iraq, Israel, Egypt, and Libya. For more than one hundred years, Persia had been trying to gobble up bits of Greece as well.

Twice, a Persian army had invaded Greece, but had been driven off both

The Persian army had already attacked Greece before Alexander was born.

times. Afterward, Persia tried to weaken Greece by bribing leaders of some city-states to wage war against others. The Greeks and their neighbors feared and hated the Persian Empire, and longed to somehow destroy its power.

Thus, Alexander was born into a world of warring barbarians, proud and freedom-loving Greeks, who also often warred with one another, and a vast and dangerous empire that seemed determined to continue on its path of conquest. War was a way of life. Wheat fields were trampled flat by marching armies, orchards of fruit trees were deliberately chopped down, towns were burned to the ground, and innocent people could suddenly be killed or turned into slaves in an instant. It was a violent and often brutal world.

2

WARFARE IN ALEXANDER'S TIME

The story of Alexander's often amazing victories and conquests begins with his father, King Philip II of Macedonia. It was Philip who created the army that Alexander led. Philip was a wild, pleasure-loving man who drank a lot of wine. However, a Macedonian king was expected to be the leader of the Macedonian Army, and Philip took that duty very seriously. He did everything he could to make the Macedonian Army as good as it could possibly be, and he was tremendously successful in his efforts.

In most of Europe at this time, battles were fought by mobs of men rushing at each other and stabbing with spears, every man for himself. But the Greeks had created a new kind of warfare. They arranged masses of men in many long rows, one behind another. The men were armed with big shields and long spears and marched in step. Thus, they created a moving wall that a mere mob of rushing men could not break through. This formation was called a phalanx.

The basis of a Greek phalanx was formed by putting 144 men together in rows—12 men across and 12 men deep.[1] Usually, four of these units were put together into an even larger phalanx of 576 men in 48 rows, 12 men deep. Units that size could then be put together to form phalanxes thousands of men strong, arranged in many different ways.

ARMOR, SPEAR, AND SHIELD

The men who formed a phalanx were called hoplites, which means heavily armored foot soldiers. A hoplite wore a thick bronze helmet that covered his head almost completely and weighed as much as five pounds. His chest was covered with either a bronze breastplate, or armor made of pieces of canvas or linen glued together and covered with thin bronze strips. Thin bronze straps, known as greaves, wound around to protect the legs from knee to ankle. In addition to his body armor, on his left arm the hoplite carried a large, round three-foot-wide shield that covered him from his chin to his knee. It was formed of a solid sheet of bronze fitted around a wooden frame. Called a hoplon, this shield was the source of the word hoplite. In his right hand the hoplite carried his main weapon, a ten-foot-long spear, whose shaft was made of a hard wood, with a two-foot-long, leaf-shaped, pointed iron blade on the end. This was a weapon for stabbing, not throwing. Hanging from the hoplite's left side was a thirty-inch-long double-edged iron sword in an iron sheath, a weapon for slashing. However, this was a "backup" weapon to which the hoplite resorted only if his spear broke. Altogether, armor, shield, spear, and sword weighed about seventy pounds. These armored hoplites, with their big shields and long spears, were called "heavy" infantry.

 ## A New Kind of Army

At the time Philip II became king, Macedonia was a backward country of a few wealthy landowners and many poor peasants who made their living by farming, herding, and hunting. The army was made up of foot soldiers, who were peasants, and cavalry, who were landowners who had horses. The foot soldiers were poorly armed and equipped and not trained to do much more than rush at their enemies, hacking and stabbing.

Philip remade the Macedonian Army. He organized the foot soldiers into phalanxes, but he made them larger than Greek ones. He increased the size of the phalanx from 144 to 256 men, 16 rows of 16 men across, a basic unit called a syntagma. He also equipped his men with longer spears than the Greeks used. The spear, called a sarissa, was about twenty-one-feet long and weighed more than seventeen

Philip of Macedonia

How a Phalanx Fought

A battle between phalanxes was simple. Phalanxes marched straight at each other across a field. At a command from their leaders they would break into a run until they just slammed together.

The men in the first four or five rows held their spears level with their heads, pointed straight ahead. Those in the rows behind moved with their spears pointed up. When two phalanxes met, a vicious shoving and jabbing match began, with the men in front trying to push each other back and stab one another. This was known to soldiers as "the push of the shields." If a man was knocked down, or hurt so that he fell down, a man in the row behind him moved forward to take his place. This kind of fighting really did not require much skill; it mainly just needed strong men who were willing to keep pushing forward!

Eventually, when one phalanx lost so many men that those left felt themselves being pushed backward, some men would turn and run away and the phalanx would begin to come apart. The men of the victorious phalanx would chase after the fleeing men, trying to stab as many as they could from behind. When the victors got too tired to run anymore, the battle was over.

pounds.[2] This meant that the soldier had to use both hands to wield it. Philip trained his Macedonian phalanxes to attack with the first five rows of men holding their spears waist high, pointing straight forward. This made them project some fifteen feet beyond the front of the phalanx, creating a wall of bristling spear points.

The men in the rest of the rows held their sarissa upright, slanting slightly forward. Those thousands of long spear shafts, projecting about fifteen feet above the heads of the men carrying them, formed a wall of defense against arrows. Many arrows would strike a shaft and simply bounce off.

Philip also created another kind of heavy infantrymen, known as hypaspists. They wore armor and helmets, and carried big shields and a spear, but they

The Macedonian phalanx intimidated many of its enemies.

were trained for hand-to-hand fighting rather than fighting in a phalanx. Their main job was guarding the king in battle.

THROWERS, ARCHERS, AND SLINGERS

Philip also made use of "light" infantry. These were mostly young men who could run fast and wore no armor to slow them down. They carried a small round or crescent-shaped shield made of stiff dried plant stems woven together and covered with leather, usually goatskin. Such a shield was called a pelta, and the soldier who carried it was called a peltast. The peltast's main weapon was a short, light spear for throwing, known as a javelin, and he generally carried two of these. He was also armed with a sword. The peltast's job was to run in close to the side of an enemy phalanx or cavalry force, throw his javelins, then

A peltast

retreat. If he was able to, he might hack with his sword at an enemy horseman or the men on the edge of a phalanx.

There was another type of light infantryman known as psiloi. These men were archers and slingers. The archer was armed with a bow and arrows, which he could use to shoot an arrow to a distance of two hundred yards. The slinger's weapon was a strap of soft leather, called a sling, and a quantity of egg-shaped, one-ounce lead missiles. The pieces of lead were cast in a mold. A slinger would put a missile in the middle of the sling, hold both ends of the sling in one hand, and whirl it rapidly in a circle over his head. By letting go of one end with a snap of his wrist, he could send the missile flying 120 yards through the air so fast it could not be seen.

At that speed, the missile could embed itself in the flesh of a man's arm or leg so that it would have to be cut out.[3] Even a man wearing a helmet could be knocked unconscious if struck in the head. Most lead missiles had inscriptions cast into them, such as "Take that!"[4]

LIGHT AND HEAVY HORSE SOLDIERS

Philip's Macedonian phalanxes had help that the Greek ones did not have. Most city-states had small cavalry forces that were only used, for the most part, for scouting an enemy force to see what they were doing, or for guarding the sides of a phalanx. But Philip built his cavalry into a force that could fight hard and help win battles. His main cavalry were "heavies," like hoplites, and wore a helmet, a breastplate of scale armor, and greaves. Their horses, too, had scale armor coverings protecting their head and chest. The main weapon of these cavalrymen was a long spear that could either be hurled or used as a lance, to stab an enemy horseman or foot soldier. They also carried short swords. The Macedonian heavy cavalry was known as "The Companions," because it was made up of landowners who were Philip's relatives and friends. He often went hunting with these men.

Philip's forces also had light cavalry. These riders wore helmets and carried shields, but wore no other armor. Their weapons were javelins and swords. Neither saddles nor stirrups had been invented at that time. The horse simply had a small blanket thrown over its back. These horses were quite small, not much bigger than a modern pony, and to mount one, a man simply jumped on its back.

PHILIP BUILDS THE BEST ARMY HIS WORLD HAS EVER SEEN

The phalanxes that formed the Macedonian Army were made up of 16 hoplite syntagmas each, totaling 4,096 men in a 16-deep line that was 800 yards wide. In front of them was a line of 1,024 psiloi, four rows deep; behind them were 2,048 peltasts, eight rows deep. At each end of the psiloi and hoplite formations was a force of 256 cavalry, four rows deep and 250 yards wide. Thus, a complete phalanx consisted of 7,168 foot soldiers and 1,024 horsemen.[5] When a Macedonian army went to war, it was generally formed of four of these phalanxes.

While most Greek city-states only called men to serve in an army when needed, Philip kept his army together at all times, as a permanent, or "standing," army. This enabled him to keep the army in constant training. He trained the troops until they could handle their weapons skillfully and change their movement quickly and smoothly.

He took them on long hard marches through all kinds of countryside in all kinds of weather so that they became used to marching long distances quickly. His soldiers became tough, hard, and confident, sure of what they could do.

Philip gave his army something no other army in the world had. He had heard of the machines that some Greek armies used to knock down the walls of cities they were trying to capture. These were ballistas, which hurled large rocks weighing as much as fifty pounds for as much as half a mile, and catapults, which were huge bows that shot giant spears for about the same distance. The Greeks built these as they needed them, right by the cities they were besieging, and just left them behind when the city was taken. But Philip hired Greek engineers to build a number of catapults and ballistas and put them in wagons pulled by horses, so he could take them along with his army anywhere it went. Thus, Philip created the world's first mobile "siege train."[6]

A POWER TO BE FEARED

When Philip became king, Macedonia was nothing more than a primitive barbarian kingdom, and it was in danger of being carved into pieces by stronger barbarian kingdoms around it. Because of the poor condition of the Macedonian Army before Philip improved it, one of the Illyrian tribes, called the Dardanians, had been able to take over a large section of western Macedonia. Philip was determined to regain this part of his kingdom.

Today, if a nation goes to war, national leaders do not actually fight as part of the army. But in Philip's time, a king was expected to lead his army, and to risk his life in battle if need be. In the spring of 358 B.C., Philip set out for his first battle. He took his new army of ten thousand foot soldiers and six hundred cavalry into the invaded territory and met a Dardanian army of about the same size, spread out in a long line. It was no match for his phalanx. The Dardanians suffered seven thousand casualties, while Macedonian casualties were light.[7] When Philip demanded a peace treaty, the Dardanians quickly agreed, swore submission to Philip, and left Macedonia. The other Illyrian tribes also became very anxious to keep peace with Philip.

In less than two years, Philip had turned Macedonia into a military power that was capable of protecting itself against the barbarian tribes around it. The rise of Macedonia was also beginning to cause concern for the leaders of many of the Greek city-states.

3

ALEXANDER'S BOYHOOD

In 356 B.C., the year Alexander was born, a "holy war" broke out in Greece. The conflict was about who should control Delphi, the great holy place of Greece. Delphi was a town on the side of a mountain called Parnassus, in central Greece. It was the site of the temple to the god Apollo, the most important religious sanctuary in the country. Apollo was the Greek god of light who represented civilization, high morals, and wisdom. He was also said to be a god who helped people with prophecies. In the temple at Delphi, an oracle—a priestess who was believed to speak the words of a god— would answer questions about important matters affecting city-states or individuals. The questioners were expected to give the sanctuary a rich gift when an answer was received, so over the years the sanctuary had built up enormous wealth.

At one time, a city-state called Phocis had been responsible for looking after Delphi. Later, Delphi had come under the control of a league of a number of the city-states around it, mainly those of the region of Thessaly. However, in the summer of 356 B.C. an army of Phocians and some hired Greek mercenaries—soldiers who would fight for anyone who paid them—seized control of Delphi and its wealth. The Phocians maintained that only they had the right to control Delphi.

PHILIP ENTERS THE WAR

For the members of the Thessalian league, this was sacrilege. They decided that war should be declared on Phocis. However, Athens, Sparta, and several other city-states sided with Phocis, and a war began.

The war dragged on for several years. Then, a Phocian leader began using some of the treasure of Delphi to hire more mercenaries to make the Phocian army stronger. By 353 B.C., Thessaly was in serious danger of being overcome. Thessaly and Macedonia were neighbors and on good terms with each other. In desperation, the Thessalians appealed for help from King Philip. He quickly brought his army marching to the Thessalians' aid.

In 352 B.C., with an army of Macedonian and Thessalian troops, Philip caught the Phocian army at Crocos Plain. Philip had his soldiers wearing wreaths of laurel leaves around their helmets, as a symbol that they were defending the temple of Apollo against the Phocians who had desecrated it. Convinced that the god was with them, the Macedonians were eager to fight. Philip's Macedonian and Thessalian cavalry wiped out the Phocian cavalry. The Macedonian phalanx destroyed the Phocian infantry, inflicting six thousand casualties.[1] The Phocians were driven out of Thessaly.

Philip Worries the Greeks

In the summer of 352 B.C., Philip began marching toward Delphi, with the purpose of taking it away from the Phocians. But Athens moved to prevent this. It put together an army of men from several city-states plus mercenaries, and blocked the only pass through the mountains that Philip's army could use to get to Delphi. It was a very narrow pass, and Philip decided he could not push through it when it was so well-defended. He turned back. However, he had gained tremendous popularity in Thessaly for all the help he had given, and the Thessalians voted to make him their leader. Philip now ruled both Macedonia and Thessaly.

Many Greeks found this very disturbing. An Athenian leader by the name of Demosthenes began to make speeches to his people, warning that Philip was a great danger to Greece. "A Macedonian is triumphing over Athenians and settling the destiny of Hellas," he told them.[2]

Demosthenes was right to be worried. Philip had a great dream. He wanted to take control of Greece and lead the forces of Greece and Macedonia in a war of revenge against the Persian Empire!

Preparing to Be a Soldier

While the Sacred War was going on, Alexander was growing up and learning about his world. Most people of this ancient time believed in many gods and supernatural beings who controlled various parts of nature and the events of life, such as weather, plant growth, wisdom, and love.

Alexander's mother, Queen Olympias, was the kind of person known as a mystic, someone who believes in and performs magical ceremonies and rituals that are supposed to reveal the intentions and secrets of the gods. Thus, she was both a priestess and a would-be sorceress. She was apparently convinced that Alexander was actually the son of a god named Zeus Ammon.

When she married Philip, Olympias was a princess of the small kingdom of Epirus in the northwest part of Greece. It was generally believed that her family was descended from the legendary Greek hero-warrior Achilles, who had fought in the Trojan War a thousand years earlier. She reared Alexander to believe in the things she did, especially making sacrifices to the gods, and as a result, he grew up to be very superstitious and was convinced that he was destined to do incredible things throughout his life.

Queen Olympias was trying to rear Alexander to become a mystic, but King Philip was trying to rear him to become a soldier. While Alexander was still quite young, Philip put him in the care of a man named Leonidas, who began training him to be a horseman, swordsman, and athlete. Leonidas also took the boy on long hard marches, and made him eat only plain food such as a soldier might get, in small portions. Years later, Alexander said Leonidas had made him march half the night to give him an appetite for breakfast, and then made him eat a light breakfast to build his appetite for dinner![3] When Alexander would receive packages from his mother, Leonidas went through them to make sure she had not sent Alexander any fancy food.

THE SCHOOL OF ROYAL PAGES

In 342 B.C., when he was fourteen, Alexander entered the School of Royal Pages. In ancient and medieval times, a page was a boy who acted as a servant for a king or other nobleman. Alexander was one of about fifty boys, sons of noble Macedonian families, who for the next four years lived together and were educated together, while they attended to some of King Philip's needs. They guarded the king while he slept, held his horse while he mounted, rode with him when he hunted, and fought beside him if he went to war. It was among these boys that Alexander made lifelong friends who would be with him in all or most of his battles: Ptolemy, who became one of his generals; Nearchus, who became an admiral; and Hephaestion, Alexander's closest friend.

The pages were actually being trained to become commanders of the Macedonian Army, so a lot of their time was spent learning to use weapons and making themselves strong and hardy. They exercised, ran races against one another, wrestled, and competed with different kinds of weapons. According to the stories about him, Alexander was the best at almost all these things. He was an excellent archer, a fine swordsman, a speedy runner, and a skillful hunter.

Apparently, the boys looked forward to the future and hoped to become great conquerors. King Philip was probably a role model for all of them. But they may have

THE STORY OF ALEXANDER'S FAMOUS HORSE

At the age of about eleven or twelve, Alexander showed that he was becoming a person of courage and determination. A Greek horse dealer brought a beautiful black horse to show the king. Philip and some of his courtiers, along with Alexander, went to the stables to look the horse over. The horse reared and kicked and showed such spirit that Philip decided he could not be tamed. Philip told the  handlers to take the horse away. However, Alexander begged to be allowed to try to tame the animal, insisting he could do it. Most of the adults just laughed, but Philip finally consented.

According to the story, Alexander took the reins and led the horse around in a half-circle. That way, the horse was facing in the other direction toward the sun. The boy had noticed that the horse had probably become excited because it was looking at its own leaping, moving shadow, and now the shadow was gone. Alexander talked softly to the horse for a time, stroking his neck. Then he hoisted himself up onto the horse's back. The horse seemed perfectly willing to allow the boy to sit on him, and now seemed quite tame. The boy had shown that he had courage and determination and Philip proudly bought the horse for him. The horse was named Bucephalus, meaning "ox head," and from then on he was Alexander's steed. Alexander became an extremely skillful horseman.[4]

feared that he would not leave anything for them to conquer. It was said that Alexander told them that his father would get everything done before they were ready and would leave them no chance of doing anything great or important![5]

A SPECIAL TEACHER

At first, Alexander had a tutor named Lysimachus, who taught him to read and write and do some arithmetic. But sometime in 342 B.C., King Philip invited the philosopher Aristotle to come to Macedonia and take over Alexander's education. King Philip told Alexander that he wanted him to have a good education so that Alexander would not "do a great many things of the sort

THE WISDOM LOVERS OF GREECE

In Greece at this time, there were a number of men who were known as philosophers. This comes from two Greek words meaning "wisdom" and "lover," so philosophers were "wisdom lovers."

Most people in the world then simply accepted the way things were, but philosophers wanted to find out about almost *everything*. They wanted to know what the sun, moon, and stars were, what fire was, how the world had come about, why things fell down and never up, why people got sick. One philosopher, Democritus, once said that he would rather find clear proof for the cause of something than be king of Persia.[6]

that I am sorry to have done."[7] Aristotle was not well-known at this time, but in later years he became famous throughout Greece, and eventually he became well-known all over the world.

Today, Aristotle is regarded as one of the greatest thinkers of the western world, which at this time consisted of Europe and all the nations settled and created by Europeans. One of Aristotle's greatest ideas was the use of logic, a way of carefully thinking things out according to certain rules. He taught Alexander how to do this. He also taught Alexander to become "a lover of learning and a lover of reading," according to the ancient historian Plutarch.[8]

Alexander's famous teacher was Aristotle. Aristotle was the student of Plato, another philosopher. Plato had been the student of Socrates, one of the greatest Greek philosophers. So, in Aristotle, Alexander really benefited from three generations of Greek wisdom.

In his late teens and early adult years, he showed that he could be different from his father. He drank wine only very sparingly and did not care for wild parties. He loved books and reading. Aristotle had taught him to be interested in things Philip paid no attention to.

ALEXANDER'S FIRST VICTORY

In 340 B.C., Philip decided to conquer part of Thrace. He would be gone from Macedonia for many months, perhaps even years. He needed someone he could depend on to take care of his kingdom. He picked Alexander, who was then sixteen years old, and appointed him regent, with the power to rule Macedonia in Philip's name. This meant that Philip was selecting Alexander to be king after him, when he died.

As regent, Alexander carried out the daily duties of a king with care. Such duties were normally fairly simple. But suddenly, something occurred that required him to use his judgment and courage for the good of the kingdom. The Maedi, one of the barbarian Illyrian tribes that owed allegiance to Macedonia, rose in revolt. As acting king, Alexander took command of the portion of the Macedonian Army that Philip had left behind and led it against the barbarians. Alexander defeated the Maedi in a battle and captured their main city. He forced all Maedians to leave and opened the city up to Macedonians and Greeks who wished to live there, renaming it Alexandropolis, "Alexander's City." Alexander had shown that he had the ability to act instantly, the courage to command Macedonian forces in battle, and the military skill to win.

ALEXANDER BECOMES KING

Alexander had his eighteenth birthday in 338 B.C. He and all the other pages of the same age had graduated. Alexander continued his duties as regent, but he must have wondered what the future held for him.

He soon found out. Philip was winning battles in Thrace, and his conquests there were of great concern to the Athenians. Demosthenes finally convinced the Athenians that they had to fight Philip to preserve their freedom. Athens quickly made alliances with Thebes and several other city-states and hired a force of mercenaries. War was declared on Macedonia. Philip sent word to Alexander to come to him.

The Athenians felt sure Philip would march south and attack them. The Athenian army took up a position guarding some mountain passes that led into the regions of Attica, the land controlled by Athens, and Boeotia, controlled by Thebes. Philip would have to come through one of these passes to get to Athens and Thebes.

One of the passes was being guarded by about ten thousand Greek mercenaries. As time went on and nothing happened, they grew careless and stopped taking precautions. Suddenly, Philip brought his army smashing into them one night, and virtually wiped them out. With their flank, or side, now open to attack, the rest of the Greeks pulled back to Boeotia. There, they formed a line of battle on a plain called Chaeronea, and waited.

THE BATTLE OF CHAERONEA

The mile-long Greek line stretched across the plain from a river to the foot of a rocky hill. The Greek line was made up of thirty thousand Athenian, Theban, and Corinthian hoplites. Many of these men were mercenaries. The army that Philip moved toward them consisted of about thirty-thousand Macedonian foot soldiers and two thousand Macedonian horsemen.[1] Philip had command of the foot soldiers, but he had given command of the horsemen to Alexander.

The battle, known as the Battle of Chaeronea, took place in August of 338 B.C. The left side of the Greek line was formed of ten thousand Athenian foot soldiers. Confident of victory, they began to push forward. Philip ordered the part of his army facing the Greek line to slowly pull back, as if retreating. As the Athenians followed, a gap opened up between them and the rest of the Greek force, which now had an open, unprotected flank. Alexander suddenly launched a cavalry charge into this gap and slammed into the unprotected foot soldiers. The Greek line began to come apart.

A MACEDONIAN VICTORY

Philip quickly ordered his withdrawing foot soldiers to halt their pullback and move forward to attack the Athenians. The long Macedonian spears reached into the Athenian phalanx and the shorter Greek spears could not fight them off. Athenians began to fall, the Athenian phalanx crumpled, and the rest of the Greek army dissolved, with thousands of men running away or surrendering. A thousand Athenians were killed, and thousands more were wounded and captured.[2] The Thebans also took heavy losses at the hands of the fierce Macedonian forces.

Philip treated all the defeated Greek city-states very mercifully, except for the Thebans. He regarded them as traitors, because even though he had a peace treaty with them, they had fought against him. Thebes was forced to give up some territory and had to submit to having a large unit of Macedonian soldiers stationed in the city. But most of the other Greeks were well-treated. Those taken prisoner were released instead of being sold into slavery as was usually done. The bodies of dead soldiers were burned, and Philip had Alexander take the ashes of all the Athenians back to Athens. This was a mark of great respect that the Athenians appreciated.

THE GREEKS AGREE TO A WAR AGAINST THE PERSIAN EMPIRE

The Athenians and other Greeks defeated at Chaeronea expected Philip to demand payments of money, plots of land, and promises of loyalty, which is what they would have done if they had won. They were astounded when instead he suggested that a conference of all the major Greek powers should be held, to discuss ways of ending the constant warfare between city-states that was tearing Greece apart. Most Greek leaders agreed.

The conference was held in the city of Corinth. Philip ran the conference, but for the most part he just let the Greeks talk. Finally, however, he made a speech urging that instead of fighting among themselves, all Greeks should band together with Macedonia and wage a war of vengeance against the Persian Empire. He suggested that he should be named captain-general—highest commander—of all Greek and Macedonian forces.

Most Greeks were eager for revenge against the Persian Empire for its two invasions. They realized that Philip, who had won all his battles against barbarians as well as Greek armies, was the best man to be in charge of a war against the Persians. With the exception of Sparta, all the city-states agreed to stop fighting among themselves, to go to war with the empire, and to make Philip captain-general. Calling themselves "the Greek League," the city-states swore an alliance with Philip "and his descendants"[3] for all time. Philip had achieved his dream of becoming the commander of a Macedonian-Greek army that would invade Persia.

An Insult, an Explosion of Anger

Up until now, everything had been going very well between Philip and Alexander. It seemed obvious that Philip intended that Alexander would be the next king of Macedonia after him, but soon events began to cast doubt on that. Macedonian kings could have more than one wife, and Alexander's mother, Olympias, was the seventh woman Philip had married.

Inasmuch as she was his last wife, Olympias was officially the queen of Macedonia. But in 337 B.C., Philip fell in love with a young Macedonian girl, and made her his eighth wife. This meant she was now the queen of Macedonia. It was a bitter blow for Olympias, and probably for Alexander as well.

The girl, whose name was Cleopatra, was the niece of one of Philip's bodyguards, a Macedonian man named Attalus. There was a great feast after the wedding, and, as generally happened, most of the men drank a lot of wine. At one point, Attalus got unsteadily to his feet and called out to everyone to pray for Cleopatra to have a baby boy who would be a true heir to the throne of Macedonia.

This was a terrible insult to Alexander! It meant that Attalus thought he was not fit to become king of Macedonia. This may have been because he was not a full-blooded Macedonian—his mother was an Epirote. According to stories that have come down to us,

Alexander threw his wine goblet at Attalus's head. Attalus ducked and hurled his own wine goblet back at Alexander.[4]

A Rift Between Father and Son

At this time in Macedonia and Greece, people at parties did not sit on chairs to eat and drink. They reclined on couches. According to the stories of what happened next, Philip began to get up from his couch, pulling his sword from its sheath. But his crippled leg gave way, and he fell, sprawling on the floor. Alexander stepped forward and stood over Philip for a moment. He then sneered, saying that this was a man who wanted to cross from Europe to Asia but could not even get from one couch to another.[5] Then he turned and strode from the room.

None of this may actually have happened. But for whatever reason, relations became strained between Alexander and his father. The morning after these events, Alexander and his mother left the city together.

Philip began to make plans for the invasion of Asia Minor, a peninsula that projects out of southwestern Asia toward Greece, between the Black Sea and Mediterranean Sea. Today, it is occupied by a large part of the nation of Turkey. In Philip's time, it was part of the Persian Empire.

Philip sent a force of about ten or twelve thousand troops to the coast of Asia Minor to set up what soldiers call a "bridgehead," a well-guarded and defended place on a coast where an army can safely land.

Philip was now ready to take the army across the Hellespont and begin his war of conquest. But first he had some family business to take care of. He gave permission for one of his daughters to marry the king of Epirus. The marriage took place in October of 336 B.C. It was an important, royal event, arranged to last several days. On the first day there was a large, lavish feast, attended by many guests. The second day there was to be a religious drama in a theater. As it turned out there was a drama, but it was very unexpected.

A Murder

Philip entered the theater with his seven bodyguards in line behind him. Inside, the bodyguards spread out and Philip walked forward alone. Suddenly, one of the bodyguards, a young man named Pausanius, darted after Philip and stabbed him in the back with a dagger! Three of Philip's other bodyguards rushed at Pausanius with shouts of rage. He began to run toward a group of horses standing near an entrance at the far end of the theatre, but stumbled and went sprawling. Instantly, the other three men were upon him and stabbed him to death with their spears. However, Philip was dead and Macedonia suddenly had no king.

For a time there was shock and confusion. Macedonia did not have any law covering who would become king when a king died. It was up to the nobles, the generals, and other leaders to pick someone. But in this case, the choice of a new king was obvious. The army liked Alexander and respected him. Philip's two best

WHY WAS PHILIP ASSASSINATED?

Mystery surrounded Philip's assassination. Why had Pausanius killed the Macedonian leader? It looked very much as if there had been a plot to get Philip out of the way so someone could steal the throne of Macedonia. Over the centuries, some historians have claimed that Alexander and his mother, Olympias, were actually behind the assassination. Today, most historians feel there is no evidence for this. It seems that Pausanius may simply have hated Philip because he felt Philip had not properly punished some men who had wronged him. However, Alexander ordered an investigation and, in time, a number of people were executed for treason. One of these was Attalus, the father of Philip's most recent wife, Cleopatra, and the man Alexander had quarreled with. Both Cleopatra and her baby were also put to death, possibly by some of Alexander's supporters who might have felt the woman and child represented a threat to Alexander's kingship. Many people believed that Olympias was responsible for the murder of Cleopatra and her baby.[6]

and most loyal generals, Parmenio and Antipater, announced their support for Alexander. When Alexander's name was announced at the meeting held to select a new king, the soldiers showed their preference by clashing their spears against their shields. At the age of twenty, Alexander was king of Macedonia. He became known as Alexander III, because there had been two other Macedonian kings with his name before him.

5

BATTLING
BARBARIANS

With the death of Philip, Macedonia's enemies erupted in revolt and defiance. They were not afraid of Alexander as they had been of Philip. Demosthenes assured the Athenians that Alexander was of no importance and urged that the alliance between members of the Greek league and "Philip's descendants" be ignored. In Thebes and several other Greek city-states, there was talk of dropping out of the league. In Thessaly, people who had been against Philip's control of Thessaly seized power and sent troops to guard the mountain passes between Thessaly and Macedonia.

Alexander knew that unless he acted instantly, the Greek league would completely come apart and it would be the end of all hope to invade Persia. He also knew that the army his father had left him could probably beat any Greek army. He set out to regain Greece.

The way into Greece was through Thessaly, but the way into Thessaly was blocked by Thessalian troops at the mountain passes. To make an attack on a strongly

43

defended mountain pass was too much of a risk, so Alexander had to find another way. He put his troops on ships and sailed along the mountainous coast of Thessaly, on the Aegean Sea, until they were past the region where the passes were. They put ashore, and Alexander set his men to work actually hacking a flight of stairs up the side of a mountain! When this was finished, the army climbed to the top of the mountain and was in Thessaly.

ALEXANDER CONQUERS GREECE WITHOUT A BATTLE

When the Thessalians learned that a Macedonian army was in their country, they were astounded—and terrified. Alexander could now have marched through the land destroying every city if he had wanted to, and the Thessalians knew it. But Alexander wanted Thessaly's help, not its hatred. He called a meeting of Thessalian leaders and requested that they give him the same position, respect, and help they had given his father. They agreed. They also gave him a large force of Thessalian heavy cavalry, the best in Greece.

With the way now open, Alexander marched down into the rest of Greece. He called a meeting of the league of city-states that looked after Delphi. He asked that he be named captain-general of all Greece, as his father had been. Impressed by his nerve and by his army, the league agreed.

However, Athens and Thebes had not sent representatives to the meeting. It looked as if they intended to ignore Alexander, who immediately marched toward Thebes. Both Thebes and Athens quickly sent representatives to him, apologizing and asking for forgiveness. Alexander very courteously and graciously accepted the apologies and assured the cities they were forgiven. Then he marched to Corinth.

At Corinth, Alexander sent messengers out to all city-states to send representatives to a meeting. Everyone in Greece was frightened of him now, so every city except big, powerful Sparta sent representatives. With most of the Greeks gathered together, Alexander made a speech urging them to appoint him, as they had his father, captain-general of a Greek and Macedonian force that would invade the Persian Empire. He had shown that he was just as capable and as dangerous as Philip had been, and he received a unanimous vote. Without fighting a single battle, losing a single soldier, or killing a single Greek, Alexander had literally conquered Greece.

A WELCOME PROPHECY

With Greece under control, Alexander felt he could turn his attention to the other places where trouble had flared up after Philip's death. In Thrace, there was a barbarian tribe known as the Triballi, living along the Danube River northwest of Macedonia, in what today is the country of Bulgaria. Now they were causing trouble on the Macedonian border. In the northeast, two Illyrian tribes, the Dardanians and Taulantians, had invaded northern Macedonia. Alexander could not allow these

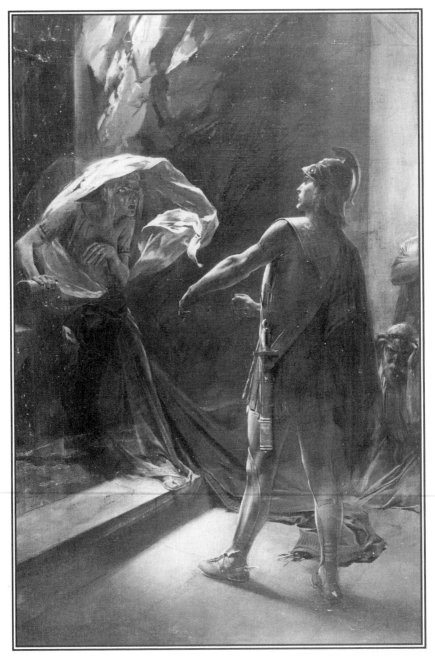

During Alexander's time, most Greeks and Macedonians believed the things an oracle said. This is why Alexander sought the oracle's advice at Delphi.

threats to Macedonia to continue. He started marching the Macedonian Army back home.

On the way, he decided to stop at Delphi and ask the oracle to give him a prophecy that would tell if his planned invasion of the Persian Empire would be successful. However, at Delphi he was told that it was one of the days that was not favorable for the oracle to give prophecies. Alexander was not one to give up, so he went to the house where the oracle lived and requested a special prophecy. It is not known whether he simply talked the elderly woman into doing so, or whether, as one ancient writer claimed, he grabbed her by the arm and started to drag her to the temple. At any rate, she gave in. "My son," she told him, "you are invincible [unbeatable]!"[1] This was good enough for Alexander. As far as he was concerned, she had prophesied that he would conquer Asia.

THE TRIBALLI MAKE A PLAN THAT ALEXANDER SPOILS

In the spring of 335 B.C., Alexander set out with his army, determined to deal with the Triballi first and then take care of the Illyrians. He headed into Thrace.

The Triballi were not at all equipped to fight a Macedonian phalanx. Their weapons were mainly daggers and spears that they used for hunting, and most of them had no armor. But learning that Alexander was coming, Triballi leaders came up with what seemed like a good plan. To get into their territory, Alexander's army would have to go through a pass in the mountain range now known as the Balkans, which run through Bulgaria. On the slopes of the pass, the Triballi brought together all the wooden farm wagons they could find. The idea was that as the phalanx moved up the slope, the Triballi would roll scores of wagons down on it.

This would cause the phalanx to break up, enabling the Triballi warriors to rush in and attack the Macedonians, who would be at a disadvantage. Their long, heavy sarissas would be useless in close man-to-man combat.

However, as the Macedonians neared the pass, Alexander saw what the Triballi were preparing to do and instantly worked out a defense against it. He halted the army and explained to his soldiers what he wanted

In Thrace, Alexander's phalanx of soldiers was able to avoid speeding wagons, and the Tribilli force was quickly put down by the Macedonian sarissas.

them to do. Then the phalanx continued forward and began to move up the slope.

The Triballi men began to push scores of wagons rumbling down the hill. As the wagons rolled toward them, the rows of Macedonian hoplites simply moved to the right and left as necessary, forming lanes that the wagons just rolled on through. Men who could not move out of the way lay down flat, covered themselves with their shields, and let the wagons roll over them. While some men suffered broken bones, no one was killed, and the phalanx was able to quickly reform itself and continue up the slope.

Two Quick Defeats

Alexander ordered his archers to move forward on the right and pour arrows into the Triballi, who were watching the phalanx approach, dismayed by the failure of their plan. Alexander led his force of hypaspists around on the left. As the phalanx slammed into the barbarians in front, the hypaspists crashed into their right flank and the archers sprayed arrows from the left.

Overwhelmed, the Triballi suffered fifteen hundred casualties and the rest fled.[2] They left behind most of the women and children they had brought to watch them destroy the Macedonian Army. These were taken prisoner and marched to the coast under guard. There, they were put aboard ships and taken to Macedonia where they were sold as slaves.

The Macedonian Army now marched into the land of the Triballi. After a few days, scouts reported a large force of Triballi warriors preparing to make camp for the night in a narrow valley surrounded by trees. Alexander halted the phalanx and sent his archers and slingers into the woods to rain missiles on the barbarians. As he had foreseen, the Triballi chased the archers and slingers out of the woods. As the Triballi came bursting out from among the trees, the Macedonian cavalry attacked them from both sides and Alexander led the phalanx smashing into them in the middle. The Triballi fled, leaving three thousand casualties behind.[3] Macedonian losses were eleven cavalrymen and forty foot soldiers.[4]

CROSSING THE DANUBE RIVER

Three days later, Alexander reached the bank of the Danube River, where a small fleet of Macedonian warships he had ordered there were waiting. The Triballi warriors, as well as women and children and a force of other Thracians, had taken refuge on an island in the river. In addition, a large force of four thousand horsemen and ten thousand foot soldiers of the Getae, a tribe allied to the Triballi, was encamped across the river.

Alexander decided to attend to the Getae first. If he could drive them away, the Triballi and Thracians on the island would probably surrender. Of course, to deal with the Getae, he had to get his army across the river. His ships were too small and too few to carry enough men, so he would have to find another way.

The army had a great many animal hides that the soldiers used as tent covers. Alexander had the men fill them with dried grass and tie them together to form floats that men could hang on to as they swam across the river. He also had a number of rafts constructed out of logs. On a midsummer night in 335 B.C., he put fifteen hundred horsemen and four thousand infantry on the other side of the Danube.[5]

THE GETAE ASK FOR PEACE

The Getae were warriors but they were not soldiers. They did not think of such things as sentries (guards) and observation posts, so there was no one to report the Macedonian landing. Alexander had sent scouts to look for the best landing place. The landing was made near a wheat field, where the wheat was so high it hid the men as well as riderless horses. The army began to move at once, and by daybreak the foot soldiers were in phalanx formation with the river protecting their left side and the horsemen, led by Alexander, protecting their right. The Getae were astounded to see an army coming at them, and despite outnumbering the Macedonians, they fled.

Alexander's cavalry pursued them. The Getae fled to their city, which was about four miles from the river, but they made no attempt to defend it. Taking their women and children with them, they headed for the mountains. Alexander had his men collect everything of value that the Getae left behind, then they burned the city to the ground.

The Macedonian Army returned to the river and crossed back to the other side. The Triballi and Thracians on the island soon learned what had happened. Before long, ambassadors from the Triballi

king and Thracian leader came to Alexander with
presents and messages begging for peace and friendship.
Alexander felt no need to punish the barbarians any
further. He believed they had learned their lesson and
would cause no more trouble. His work in the Balkans
was finished, and he was now ready to deal with the
rebellious tribes in Illyria.

A VICTORY, A CITY'S DEMISE

It was now late summer, 335 B.C. As his army began the march to Illyria, Alexander learned that the Dardanians had seized the Macedonian town called Pelium, on the border between Illyria and Macedonia. Pelium was an important town. It was fortified, with a wall around it, a river running past it, and it stood in the only gap in a mountain range that separated Macedonia from Illyria. Whoever held the town controlled the gap. With the town in Illyrian hands, Illyrians were free to come through the gap, and western Macedonia was in constant danger of invasion.

Alexander made camp and began preparations to assault the city. Seeing this, the Dardanians, in typical barbarian fashion, killed three young boys, three girls, and three black goats, as a sacrifice to the gods, and came marching down out of the hills.

Alexander led his phalanx to meet them. There are no accounts of the battle, but the phalanx apparently made very short work of the barbarians and they were soon fleeing into Pelium, where they shut themselves in. Alexander immediately put the town under siege. This meant surrounding the town so that no one could get in or out, which would keep the people inside from getting any food or supplies. He had his men construct walls of dirt, wood, and stone outside the city's wall to protect the attackers from arrows shot from the wall by the town's defenders. Now, the Macedonians could try to batter part of the wall down with catapults and ballistas, or smash a gate open with a battering ram. Or, they could simply wait until the people inside began to starve and asked to surrender.

DAZZLING THE BARBARIANS

Before the Macedonians could do much, the Taulantian army arrived and took up a position behind Alexander on the heights around Pelium. Alexander pulled his forces back into his camp and considered what to do. He was actually in a rather bad situation. He was now seriously outnumbered. His line of retreat into Macedonia was cut off by the Taulantians, and his army was running out of food for both men and horses. If he ordered an assault on the town, the Taulantians could attack him from the rear. If he tried attacking the Taulantians on the heights, the Dardanians could come out of the city and hit him in the flank.

Alexander now did something that seems to be a mark of genius. No other general had done anything like it. With the Dardanians and Taulantians watching and waiting to see what he would do, he put his army into a giant phalanx formation, 100 men to a line, 120 lines deep, with a force of 200 cavalry on each side. Then the army began a formal military drill!

Today, military drill is done mainly for parades. But in Alexander's time, it was a way for soldiers to practice the movements they would need in a battle, until they could do them quickly and smoothly, almost without thinking. It was also a way of making troops look impressive and *fearsome* to enemy soldiers. They learned to march in step, their thousands of feet striking the ground all together, with a steady *thud, thud, thud* that shook the earth. They learned to change direction or change the position of their weapons in an instant, on command.

Alexander's soldiers knew exactly what to do as they began to drill in front of the staring barbarians. Except for the sound of their feet thudding into the earth, they moved in a menacing, unnerving silence, as Alexander had ordered. A trumpet blared, and at once all the Macedonians wheeled and were facing in another direction. Another blare, and they lowered their sarissas to the attack position in a single movement and marched forward toward a section of the barbarian line.

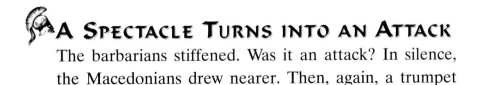

A SPECTACLE TURNS INTO AN ATTACK

The barbarians stiffened. Was it an attack? In silence, the Macedonians drew nearer. Then, again, a trumpet sounded. Instantly, the phalanx wheeled and was marching in a different direction.

The barbarians had no idea what was going on. They were brave men and good fighters, but they had never been taught to move in unison in such a way as the Macedonians were doing. They must have realized that these men would be able to move instantly and forcefully in battle.

Alexander continued to move his men through an elaborate drill. The barbarians were totally confused. Thus, when Alexander finally made his move, it was completely unexpected. The phalanx began to move toward a section of the Dardanian force as it had several times before. But instead of wheeling in another direction as it had done previously, there was a sudden scream of trumpets and, obeying their command, the phalanx instantly broke into a dead run in perfect step. At the same instant, from thousands of throats came the blood-curdling, howling yell of the Macedonian war cry—"Alalalalai!"[1] At that sound, and at the sight of those thousands of glittering sarissa-points coming straight at them, the barbarians suddenly realized this was a real attack. They turned and rushed back toward the safety of Pelium.

Seeing that the phalanx was now facing away from them, the Taulantians began to move forward to attack it from the rear. However, at a command, the phalanx wheeled and headed for them. They, too, broke and ran, rather than try to face this quick-moving, overwhelming Macedonian force.

CREATING A NEW BATTLE TACTIC

Alexander had now pushed his enemies out of the way on two sides, leaving a clear path for his troops. He sent the phalanx across the river, at a fording place where the men could wade through the water. But this was a slow process, and it gave the Taulantians a chance to regroup and start moving forward to try again to attack the phalanx from the rear.

Once again, Alexander now showed his ability to do something new, different, and totally unexpected. He had with him a number of the catapults and ballistas his father had built for use to batter down city walls, but Alexander now had them set up, clustered together, and used them against *troops*! As the Taulantians rushed forward to attack the Macedonian rear, they ran into a rain of artillery—big heavy stones and giant spears that each took out whole groups of men.

Surprised and terrified by this new type of warfare, the barbarians drew back. Alexander was able to get his whole army over the river without losing a single man. He was the first general to use artillery in this way.[2]

What Alexander had done was really remarkable. He had managed to make his opponents awed and fearful of his army's power by demonstrating its superb ability to make battle movements. He had caught his stunned opponents by surprise even though his army was in full view.

He had opened up the line of retreat into Macedonia and was now free to send troops into the nearby countryside to forage for food. However, he was not through with the Illyrians. He still had to regain control of Pelium.

A SURPRISE ATTACK

Alexander pulled his forces back slightly so they could not be seen. Then he sent scouts out to spy on the enemy troops. Three days later the scouts reported that the Illyrians were apparently under the impression that the Macedonians had completely withdrawn. They were camped in front of Pelium, badly spread out and with no sentries and no walls or ditches to help prevent an attack.

This was a perfect situation made for Alexander. That night he recrossed the river with his hypaspists, a phalanx of 768 men, and his archers and javelin throwers. Most of the Illyrians were sound asleep and when Alexander's troops came charging in from one side of the camp; the sleepers were caught completely by surprise. Hundreds were slaughtered, hundreds more captured, and the rest fled.

The Illyrians were defeated and disgraced. Alexander had now wiped out all thought of revolt by any of the barbarian tribes. However, he soon learned that uprisings against him and Macedonia were flaring up in other places. Rumor had it that he had been killed in one of the recent battles, and Thebes had declared open revolution against Macedonia. Thebans had killed several of the Macedonian soldiers stationed in their city and surrounded the part of the city where the soldiers stayed. Thebes announced its independence from Macedonia.

AN OFFER AND AN ATTACK

Other city-states rushed to join the Thebans. Forces from Argos, Arcadia, and Elis started marching to aid Thebes. Athens sent a supply of weapons and began getting its army ready to march.

When Alexander heard of all this he moved at once, marching his army at top speed in what is known as a "forced march" that covered the three hundred miles from Pelium to Thebes in thirteen days. When the Macedonian force suddenly appeared before the city as if it had dropped out of the sky, the Thebans were horror-struck.

The Argives, Arcadians, and Elisians learned that that the Macedonian army was at Thebes. Alexander's enemies halted their march and turned around to hurry home. The Athenians could not call their weapons shipment back, but they gave up all thought of sending an army to help Thebes, and waited to see what would happen. By acting as swiftly as he had, Alexander had prevented a coalition of enemy forces from forming that could have forced him to fight a dangerous battle against heavy odds.

Thebes was a heavily fortified city with thick walls, and the Thebans also had erected log fences in several places outside the wall. Alexander gave the Thebans a chance to send emissaries to ask for a pardon. His army camped outside the city and waited. Instead, the Thebans sent out some cavalry and peltasts and tried to attack Alexander's camp. They were pushed back, of course, and retreated back into the city. Despite this,

Alexander still waited. He sent word into the city that if the Thebans would give up the ringleaders who had started the rebellion, he would pardon the rest of the citizens. Most of the citizens wanted to accept these terms, but the leaders refused.

The Destruction of Thebes

Alexander drew up plans for an attack on the city, but still held off. However, one of his commanders, Perdiccas, thinking he saw a chance to break into the city, led a force of hoplites through the log fences. He was quickly joined by another commander, Amyntas, who had his troops follow. Seeing that part of his army was making a major onslaught, Alexander moved quickly in support.

Alexander had gained some allies when he marched on Thebes. For decades, Thebes had dominated and bullied the other city-states of Boeotia, and some of them—Platea, Phocis, Thespiae, and Orchomenos—had sent troops to help Alexander in any attack he might make on the city. These troops eagerly joined in the attack, and fought hard, inspired by their hatred of Thebans. The fighting raged through the streets of the city and only stopped when the remaining Theban infantry and cavalry managed to escape out of the city. Some six thousand Thebans were killed and about five hundred Macedonians and some of the allied troops.[3]

Alexander left it to his Boeotian allies to decide the fate of Thebes. Angry at the city that had humiliated them for so long, the Boeotians requested that all surviving Thebans—about thirty thousand people, mainly women and children—be sold into slavery, and that the city then be burned to the ground. Alexander agreed, decreeing that only the temples and the home of a famous poet be spared. According to one story of the destruction, it was carried out to the music of flutes, played by Macedonian Army musicians.[4]

Thebes was totally destroyed, left in smoking ruins. This was a terrifying lesson for the rest of Greece. The Athenians prepared for a similar fate, but hopefully sent emissaries to beg Alexander to spare Athens. He had no wish to destroy the city, which he admired, and he also wanted to use the big Athenian navy to take his army to Persia, so he graciously agreed not to punish Athens.

Alexander now virtually ruled Greece. Except for large and powerful Sparta, every city-state was either an actual ally or so completely under Macedonia's domination that it had no choice but to do what Alexander demanded.

7

Invasion of an Empire

In the spring of 334 B.C., Alexander left his father's old general, Antipater, as regent in Macedonia with nine thousand troops, to keep an eye on the Greek cities and the barbarians. Then, Alexander led a combined Macedonian and Greek army of about thirty thousand infantry and five thousand cavalry to the banks of the Hellespont, or Dardanelles.

At its narrowest point, the Dardanelles is only one mile wide, from the European side to the Asian. To take the army across this narrow strip of water, Alexander had brought together 182 of the big warships called triremes, and 38 smaller ships. A trireme was generally about 115 feet long and 12 feet wide, and although it had one large sail, most of its movement was provided by 85 oars in three rows on each side. An oar was fourteen feet long and each oar was pulled by one man. A trireme had a big bronze-covered ram on its front end, and its main

SCIENTISTS AND SEERS

Not all of the people with Alexander's army were soldiers. He also took along a number of men who would be called scientists today. Aristotle's teaching had made Alexander interested in learning about many things. He realized that there were probably animals and plants in Asia that Macedonians and Greeks had never seen or heard of, so he brought men who could study them and write about them.

There were also men with the army who were called seers. Most people of Alexander's time believed that their gods would sometimes make something happen that would foretell the future. Such an event is known as an omen. Seers were people who, it was believed, could understand, or *see*, what an omen meant. Alexander and his soldiers felt it was important to have seers with them, because an omen might reveal how to win a battle!

way of fighting was to row at an enemy ship and break it open with the ram. However, it could also be used to carry soldiers from one place to another. Athens and other Greek communities had supplied 160 triremes, while Macedonia had furnished 22 triremes and 32 smaller ships.

ALEXANDER MAKES A SIDE JOURNEY

The soldiers and horses were crowded aboard each vessel. Alexander took command of sixty Macedonian ships and put his elderly general Parmenio in command of the Greek fleet. But while Parmenio went straight across to the city of Arisbe, Alexander's fleet sailed a little to the south, toward the site of the ancient city of Troy. The story of the Trojan War, which was waged by ancient Greeks against the city of Troy nearly a thousand years before Alexander's time, was tremendously important to Alexander. He kept a copy of Homer's great poem about the war, *The Iliad*, with him at all times. Apparently, he believed that if he visited Troy and held special rituals and ceremonies to the gods there, it would help him be successful in conquering Asia. These were the sorts of beliefs that Alexander had been taught by his mother.

Halfway across the Hellespont, Alexander killed a bull as a sacrifice to Poseidon, the god Greeks and Macedonians believed controlled the sea. Then he poured wine into the sea from a goblet made of gold, and threw the goblet into the water. Ancient historians who wrote about Alexander's life and battles say that Alexander often made a sacrifice before doing something he considered important.

As the ships neared the shore of Asia Minor, Alexander was standing in the front of the first ship. He was in full armor and held a peltast spear in one hand. Greeks and Macedonians had a term for land that was gained by winning a battle; they called it "land won by the spear." As the ship entered shallow water, Alexander threw his spear toward shore in a high arc. The point thudded into the ground and the spear stood upright, quivering. In a loud voice, Alexander called out, "I accept from the gods Asia won by the spear!"[1] This was a formal announcement that he intended to conquer the Persian Empire. He then leaped out of the boat, waded the short distance to shore, and stepped onto the Persian Empire's soil.

Most of Troy was in ruins, but a temple of Athena remained there. Athena was a goddess of wisdom, and also of the part of warfare requiring wisdom, which we now call strategy and tactics. For this reason, she was very important to Alexander, and he made a sacrifice to her at the temple. He made other sacrifices and performed other rituals as well. He was hoping the gods and the spirits at Troy would take his side in the conquest of Asia.

THE PERSIAN EMPIRE—A COLLECTION OF MANY COUNTRIES

The Persian Empire was ruled by an emperor called Darius III, known as the High King. He was said to have been given the right to rule by the Persian god Ahura Mazda, who was believed to have created the earth, sky, and human beings. Any decision that Darius made was final, but he did accept advice from a number of special advisors and counselors.

The empire was divided into twenty provinces. The provinces were governed by noblemen known as satraps, who were often relatives of the emperor. The satraps were accountable to the emperor, sending a yearly "tribute" of gold, silver, richly embroidered clothing, furniture, bulls, cows, sheep, and horses, all collected as taxes from the people of the province. A nobleman appointed by the emperor, and known as the "King's Eye," kept watch over the doings of the satrap.

Most of the provinces had once been the countries of people who had been conquered by Persia—Medes, Babylonians, Egyptians, and others. Thus, there were different languages, customs, and religions throughout the Persian Empire. There was very little feeling of unity among the provinces. They were more like separate little kingdoms than regions united in a single nation.

They often had very different ways of life. In some provinces the people were settled on farms and in towns, in others they were nomads, moving from place to place on horseback. Some of these nomads were actually bandits, who made their living by raiding other provinces for food and loot. Satraps of different provinces were often jealous of one another, and this sometimes led to actual little wars between provinces.

The army of the Persian Empire was not permanent as the Macedonian Army was. The emperor had a palace guard of two thousand foot soldiers and two thousand cavalry, and a force of ten thousand foot soldiers known as "the Immortals." Each satrap had a small force of soldiers in the main city of his province, under the command of another nobleman who was directly responsible to the emperor. If a very large army had to be formed, the emperor issued an order to round up men from towns and villages in the provinces. Of course, these men were not trained soldiers, so the Persians generally hired large forces of experienced Greek mercenary soldiers to bolster their army.

Because of the vastness of the empire, the Persians had built up a network of roads. The main road, called the Royal Road, ran from a city on the coast of Asia Minor to a city in the middle part of the empire, more than 1,600 miles away, with many smaller roads branching off of it. At intervals of about fifteen miles, all along the Royal Road, were stations where horses were kept. Thus, messengers could change to a fresh horse at each station and keep moving at full speed. In this way, the High King and his satraps and other officials could keep in touch with one another fairly quickly.

ALEXANDER TAKES ACTION

The Persian leaders knew the Macedonians and Greeks were coming. Almost as soon as the ships carrying Alexander's army began to arrive, messengers were riding from the coast to bring word of the arrival to the emperor and commanders of the Persian army. Darius did not seem very concerned by Alexander's invasion. He sent a small force of cavalry to Phrygia, the province where Alexander's army was massing, but left it up to the satrap and troop commander to do what they thought best in response to Alexander's army.

The Persians held a council of war to decide how to best fight Alexander. One of the Persian generals was actually a Greek, named Memnon, commander of a force of twenty thousand hired Greek hoplites in the service of Persia. Memnon offered the Persian commanders a plan. Let Alexander land, he told them, then, as he moves inland, lay waste to the land he must pass through! Destroy the crops, drive off the livestock, burn the towns and villages. Alexander's army will begin to starve, and will have no shelter, said Memnon. Then, we can destroy his army easily, Memnon assured the Persians.

It was a good plan, and would probably have caused Alexander trouble. He was short of supplies and short of money to buy supplies. But the Persians would have no part of Memnon's plan. It seemed to them both cowardly and wasteful to destroy Persian farms and villages. Also, they simply did not want to accept any advice from a Greek. The plan they decided on was to put the Persian army in a good position, and let Alexander come at it. The Macedonian king decided to do just that.

Alexander stayed at Troy a short time, then marched to Arisbe and joined the rest of the Macedonian-Greek army. Now he received word that the Persian force was some fifty miles away to the northeast, in a strong position on a river called the Granicus. He decided to attack at once. He still had about thirty-five thousand men. However, he left a strong force to guard the coast, and took with him only the best of his troops—his Macedonian heavy infantry and cavalry, his superb Thessalian cavalry, and the tough Thracian and Illyrian light infantry. He led this army north, along the coast, heading toward the mouth of the Granicus.

The Arrangement and Look of the Persian Army

The Persian army was drawn up on the east bank of the river, waiting for him. Half of it was cavalry, about twenty thousand Asian cavalrymen from all parts of the empire—Persians, Medes, Bactrians, and others. The other half was also about twenty thousand men, Memnon's Greek mercenary foot soldiers, fighting for the Persians for pay. They were armed and armored much like Alexander's men, and would fight in a phalanx. The Persian commanders had their cavalry arranged along the river in front, with the foot soldiers in the rear. There was a small force of Persian foot soldiers on each side of the Greek mercenaries.

In appearance, Persian soldiers were very different from the Macedonians and Greeks. Persian foot soldiers wore no armor or helmets. Most of them were archers, carrying what is known as a recurved bow, which had a curve above and below the handgrip. With this kind of bow they could shoot an arrow up to two hundred yards. They wore a round cloth cap of dyed material, with a broad flap that hung down in back and a narrow flap hanging in front of each ear.

The earflaps were often tied together under the chin. They wore long, loose tunics that reached halfway to the knee, and long loose trousers, reaching to the ankle. A vestlike sleeveless garment of canvas that reached to the waist was worn on top of the tunic, serving as a kind of light armor. For the most part, the clothing of these common soldiers was an off-white or gray.

Persian cavalrymen wore no helmets, but some wore long-sleeved coats of armor scales, made of iron, bronze, hard leather, or animal horns. They wore the same kind of cap, tunic, and trousers as foot soldiers. They did not carry shields. They were generally armed with two short spears that could be used either for throwing or jabbing. Some carried recurved bows. The clothing of both infantry and cavalry commanders was rich and colorful, a rainbow of red, blue, pale green, purple, and yellow.

ALEXANDER ATTACKS

Alexander divided his army into two wings, or sections. On the left wing was a 4,500-man Macedonian phalanx, as well as 2,400 heavy cavalry and 150 Thracian light cavalry. This force was led by old Parmenio. Alexander commanded the right wing, formed of another 4,500-man Macedonian phalanx; 3,000 Macedonian heavy infantry; the 1,800-strong companion cavalry; 150 Paeonian light cavalry; and a 1,000-man force of Thracian archers and javelin throwers.[2] Alexander was in full armor that glittered in the sunlight. His gleaming golden helmet was topped with a large white plume. There was no mistaking who he was, and he was deliberately calling attention to himself. He wanted his soldiers to be able to see him, to see that he was leading them. However, the Persians knew who he was, too. The Persian leaders pointed at him, and talked among themselves. They felt that if they could reach Alexander and kill him, they would win the battle.

Leading the right wing, Alexander took his troops into the river and toward the bank where the Persian cavalry waited. Now, one of the improvements that Alexander's father Philip had made in the Macedonian Army really showed its worth. Had the Macedonian phalanx soldiers been armed with a ten-foot spear, as Greek hoplites were, they would never have made it out of the river. The Persian horsemen would have rained javelins down on them. But with their twenty-one-foot-long sarissas, the Macedonians could reach out and push the Persians off their horses, then stab them. The Persian cavalry was forced to give ground, and the Macedonian phalanx came surging onto the riverbank like a flood of spears! Alongside them, the Macedonian companion cavalry also came splashing out of the water with Alexander at their head. The Persian cavalry swept toward them.

THE BATTLE OF THE GRANICUS

A swirling cavalry battle erupted. Alexander and one of his generals, Cleitus, and all three of the Persian commanders were in the thick of the fighting and actually got into hand-to-hand combat with one another. The Persian cavalry commander headed straight for Alexander, intent on killing him. Seeing the Persian cavalry commander coming toward him, Alexander rode at the man and stabbed him in the head with his lance, killing him instantly. Moments later, another Persian commander encountered Alexander and aimed a vicious sword blow at his head that cut into Alexander's helmet, wounding him slightly. Alexander stabbed this man in the chest with his lance, knocking him off his horse, dead. Shortly after this, another Persian general came up behind Alexander and raised his sword to make a cut at Alexander's head. Cleitus, riding behind Alexander, swung his sword to block the cut, and sliced the Persian's hand off at the wrist, still holding the sword.

As the Persian horsemen saw their commanders going down one after another, they began to lose heart. Some began to fall back, away from the pressing, thrusting Macedonians. Abruptly, the center of the Persian line collapsed as the men turned their horses and galloped away. At this, the Persian horsemen on each side also turned and fled. About a thousand Persians had been killed and many more were wounded. The Macedonians were said to have had only eighty-five cavalrymen and thirty infantrymen killed.[3]

The twenty thousand Greek mercenaries on the Persian side still stood where they had been placed. The Persian commanders had not used them. Now, some of the Greek mercenary commanders came to Alexander and offered to surrender. But Alexander would not hear of it. He felt that Greeks fighting for Persians against other Greeks, for pay, was treason. He himself led his Macedonian phalanxes and cavalry in an attack that nearly wiped out the Greek mercenary force. Alexander finally allowed two thousand of them to surrender, but they were sent back to Macedonia with their ankles shackled together by chains, as slaves. We know they spent the rest of their lives this way, because more than two thousand years later, archaeologists found some of their skeletons with the chains still in place.[4]

The province of Phrygia was now conquered. Alexander appointed one of his officers to be the new satrap and govern the province for him while he marched on. He would do this from now on in every province or city he conquered.

8

BESIEGING PERSIA

Alexander now began a march down the coast. Hundreds of years earlier this western coast of Asia Minor had been colonized by Greeks known as Ionians. Scattered through it was an alliance of twelve Greek-style city-states. Alexander's purpose was to capture all the cities that might serve as ports for the Persian navy. If he could do this, Persian ships would never be able to land troops in any of the cities to form an army behind him and threaten him from the rear. Big and powerful though the Persian navy was, it would be helpless against him without any ports.

The first city, Sardis, simply surrendered. The next city, Miletus, tried to hold out. Miletus considered itself a Greek city but it was loyal to Persia and looked upon Alexander as a barbarian. It was an important city for the Persians, for it could provide shelter and provisions to a large fleet of ships. The inner part of the city, at the edge of the water, was surrounded by a high thick wall of stone with a deep ditch around it. Troops that included Greek mercenaries defended the city.

THE CAPTURE OF TWO CITIES

The first thing Alexander did was send for his Greek fleet of 160 triremes. They took up position in the harbor. Three days later, the Persian fleet of four hundred ships arrived. With Alexander's ships blocking the way, the Persians could not land troops to help the Persian forces in the city—unless they attacked the Greek fleet and destroyed it. It looked as if a sea battle was going to take place.

Alexander decided he must take the city at once. At dawn the next day, his catapults began hurling huge rocks at the wall. Within hours, a large section was broken down and Alexander led his troops into the city. The Persian troops defending it were virtually wiped out, but Alexander spared most of the ordinary citizens. He also accepted into his army three hundred Greek mercenaries who swore allegiance to him.[1] By now, he had lost many of his own Greek soldiers, and realized it was wiser to make use of Greek mercenaries to replace his losses, rather than to wipe them out as he had done after the Battle of the Granicus.

For a few days, the Persian fleet tried to tempt Alexander's fleet into fighting, but Alexander had issued strict orders to not fight. In time, the Persians left, sailing for an island where they could get supplies. They had not been able to affect Alexander's plans in any way.

Alexander continued down the coast, with most of the cities in his path surrendering, until he reached the last city of importance, Halicarnassus. This city was well fortified and defended, with a number of strong walls, one inside another. Alexander began to work vigorously to break into the city. He moved siege towers up to the walls and began pounding the walls with battering rams. The Persians launched an assault to destroy the towers, but the Macedonians drove them back into the city. In time, the Macedonians broke in, the walls were destroyed, and the city began to burn. The Persians pulled out of the city and took refuge in some fortresses on an island in the harbor. Alexander left a few thousand soldiers to keep them imprisoned. He now controlled the entire west coast of Asia Minor.

ALEXANDER UNDOES A KNOT AND MAKES A MISTAKE

Alexander now marched inland to a city called Gordium, where he joined Parmenio and the rest of the army. There was a very old legend associated with Gordium. In a ruined palace was an old wagon with two of its parts, called the yoke and yoke-pin, held together by several knots of thick, sturdy rope, so tightly tangled together it was impossible to tell how they were tied. The legend stated that the man who could untie the knots and separate the pieces would become the "ruler of Asia."

Alexander went to look at the knots. It is not known what actually happened, but there are stories, true or not, that Alexander managed to separate the yoke and yoke-pin, and that this made most people believe he had gained the right to be the ruler of Asia.

In mid-July of 333 B.C., Alexander got news of what his Persian enemies were doing. The emperor Darius

THE LEGEND OF THE GORDIAN KNOT

There are two stories about what happened when Alexander went to look at the so-called Gordian knot. One story says that Alexander looked down at the knots for a few moments, then called out, "It makes no difference how they are untied."[2] Drawing his sword he stepped forward and with a tremendous swing cut through the knots with a single slash. The other story is that after studying the knots, he stepped forward and simply pulled the yoke-pin out of the knots, which released the yoke! Another story says there were brilliant flashes of lightning and titanic bursts of thunder that night. This, according to the seers and religious mystics accompanying the army, indicated that the gods approved of whatever Alexander had done.

had put together an enormous force and was moving toward the coast to meet the Macedonian-Greek army and destroy it. At this time, Alexander became ill with a fever, and went to bed, shaking with chills. As weeks passed and he got no better, the doctors taking care of him began to fear he would die. However, a doctor named Philip, who had a very good reputation, produced a special medicine and brought it to Alexander.

According to the story that has come down to us, Alexander had received a letter from old General Parmenio, warning him not to take any medicine Philip might give him. Parmenio believed Philip was secretly working for Darius and would try to poison Alexander.

In this painting, Alexander is about to solve the riddle of the Gordian knot.

Nevertheless, Alexander took the medicine. In three days, he was better, and in time, was completely well again. The people around Alexander believed this showed how fearless he was in facing possible death, as well as how much confidence he had in people that he trusted.

Alexander began to move his army toward the Persians. He now did something unusual—he made a mistake. He underestimated his opponent, Darius. He presumed that Darius would come toward him through a mountain pass known as the Syrian Gates, so he headed that way. But what Darius actually did was to go through a pass much farther north, which enabled him to move his army *behind* Alexander. Alexander was now in the worst position a general could possibly be in. He was deep in enemy territory with his source of supply cut off and his line of retreat blocked!

However, Alexander had supreme confidence in his army. He immediately started the army on a forced march north. It tramped seventy miles in only two days, arriving on a November night, some distance from where the Persian army was camped. Climbing to the top of a hill, Alexander saw the thousands of glowing campfires of the enemy, dotting a broad plain just beyond a river called the Pinarus. The Persian fighting force was probably about two hundred thousand strong,[3] while Alexander had no more than thirty thousand men.[4] The odds seemed overwhelming.

However, many of the Persians were actually just very young farmworkers, who had been rounded up from all over the countryside. They had no training and no experience as soldiers.

THE BATTLE OF ISSUS

In the morning, Alexander launched an attack. His phalanxes moved forward in a long line with cavalry at each end. Darius countered by sending thirty thousand horsemen and twenty thousand of the farmworker infantrymen across the river on one side.[5] Alexander sneaked his hard-fighting Thessalian cavalry around behind his phalanxes and suddenly unleashed them against the Persians who had come across the river. The young farmworkers ran away and the Thessalians overwhelmed the Persian cavalrymen. The Macedonian and Greek phalanxes began to splash across the shallow river, a long wall of glinting spear points. Alexander led his companion cavalry up the riverbank and toward the Persian center where Darius, in gorgeous robes and a colorfully ornamented chariot, was easy to see. Catching sight of Alexander coming straight at him with a force of Macedonian cavalry, the Persian emperor turned the chariot horses and sped away at the fastest gallop he could manage. The Persian army dissolved and fled in all directions. The battle was over. Because it occurred near a town called Issus, it is known as the Battle of Issus.

Macedonian troops quickly took over the abandoned camp of the Persians. In the gorgeous tent that had belonged to Darius, they found some weeping women who turned out to be Darius's wife, mother, and two daughters. Alexander sent word to them that Darius was still alive, and that they would be well treated. The wives and families of many other Persian leaders were also captured, and Alexander saw to it that they were all made comfortable and protected.

DEFEATING THE PERSIAN FLEET—ON LAND

Alexander did not pursue the Persian forces. He felt it was much more important to continue his effort to destroy the usefulness of the Persian navy by capturing all its ports. Alexander called this strategy "defeating the Persian fleet on land."[6] In the late winter of 333 B.C., he marched his army south along the coast, into the region known as Phoenicia, which was made up of what are now parts of Syria, Lebanon, and Israel. Phoenicia had a sea-trading economy and depended on its port cities. It was not part of the Persian Empire, but it was a strong ally, and its cities were expected to resist Alexander.

However, the cities of Marathus, Byblus, and Sidon all opened their gates to Alexander. But when he reached the city of Tyre, it refused to submit. Tyre was the last port city Alexander had to take in order to make the Persian fleet completely useless. He decided to put it under siege, capture it, and destroy it for use as a port.

This was not going to be an easy matter. Tyre had once been under siege for thirteen years, and the attackers had finally given up. The city was on an island about half a mile offshore, and was surrounded by thick walls 150 feet high. It had two harbors where ships could bring in supplies, and it was defended by about thirty thousand men. It even had its own small fleet of warships.

A New Way to Besiege a City

To get to the city Tyre, Alexander had to get to the island, but he had no boats. Once again he came up with a new idea. He decided to build a causeway, an artificial road, from the shore to the island.

Nothing like this had ever been done in warfare before. In January of 332 B.C., under Alexander's direction, the work began. Soldiers cut down trees and trimmed off all branches. The trunks were then pounded down into the muddy soil under the water with their tops sticking above the water. Stones by the thousands were poured between them, with plants from nearby swamps pushed among the stones to hold them in place. Men worked at this day and night. Alexander often visited them, cheering them up, handing out presents, and sometimes even carrying stones himself. In time, a stony road was reaching toward the island, above the water. It was two hundred feet wide.

The Tyrians did what they could to hinder the work. With catapults and ballistas they shot stones and arrows at the workers. They sent boats filled with soldiers to attack. To counter this, Alexander had two wooden towers built at the end of the causeway. They were filled with soldiers to fight off attacks and held catapults and ballistas to shoot back at the Tyrians.

The work went on, and the road continued to stretch forward.

A Setback, Then a Stroke of Luck

The Tyrians filled a ship with dry tree branches, tar, and bags of oil. One night they towed it toward the end of the causeway between two triremes, set it afire, and cut it loose to float forward. It smashed into the causeway, throwing flaming material in all directions. Alexander's towers caught fire and burned down.

As usual when things went wrong for him, Alexander was not discouraged. He ordered work to begin to widen the causeway so that more towers could be put on it.

Now Alexander had a stroke of luck. All the cities that had surrendered to him had ships that were part of the Persian fleet. When the commanders of those ships learned that their cities had gone over to Alexander, they decided they should no longer fight for the Persians. They left the Persian fleet, sailed to Alexander's camp, and offered their ships to him. Ships from several other cities that preferred Alexander's rule to that of the Persians also showed up. Soon, Alexander had two hundred ships to use against Tyre.

Alexander quickly put the ships to use. The water at the base of Tyre's walls was filled with loose boulders piled up there to prevent ships from getting in close. Alexander fitted ships with cranes and nets that picked up boulders from a particular part of the wall and carried them away. In this way, a section of wall was uncovered.

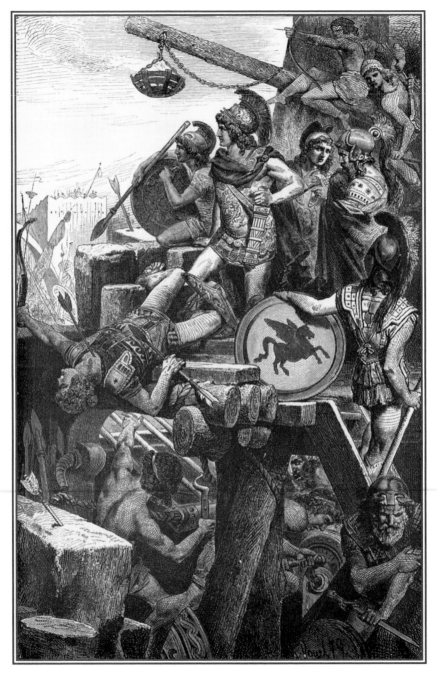

At Tyre, Alexander was once again victorious.

The Tyrians sent out almost their entire force of warships to try to prevent this, but Alexander took command of a number of Phoenician ships and showed that he could win a battle on water as well as on land. The Tyrians were driven off, with many of their ships damaged or captured.

TYRE IS CAPTURED

Alexander equipped many ships with ballistas and battering rams. They attacked Tyre's wall. After weeks of battering, a section of wall gave way. The ships that had done the battering backed away, and ships filled with Macedonian and Greek soldiers moved forward. The soldiers poured through the opening.

It had taken seven months to finally capture the city. Four hundred soldiers of Alexander's army had been killed and about four thousand wounded.[7] The Tyrians had captured some Macedonians and treated them badly, torturing them to death up on the top of the wall in full view of Alexander's soldiers. As vengeance, two thousand Tyrian men were nailed to wooden crosses along the shore and left to die. All the women and children and about thirty thousand Tyrian soldiers were sold into slavery.

9

KING OF EGYPT

From Tyre, Alexander marched 150 miles south to the city of Gaza in what is now the Palestinian area of the same name. Whoever controlled Gaza controlled the road into the land of Egypt. Alexander could have taken his army around Gaza into Egypt, but if he left the Palestinian city in Persian hands, it could be used as a base to form and supply an army that could attack him from the rear. If Gaza would not submit to him, he would have to conquer it. He sent word to the governor of the city demanding that his army be allowed to march through. Batis, the governor, refused.

THE CAPTURE OF "THE STRONG"

Thus, Alexander was faced with another siege and assault on a city. It did not seem that this would be any easier than Tyre had been. Gaza stood on a 250-foot-high hill, and was completely surrounded by a high, thick wall. The height of the hill made it extremely difficult to push siege towers up to the wall. The very name of the city meant "the strong."[1] Alexander's engineers told him it would be impossible to take the place by assault.

This only made Alexander more determined. He had his whole army, as well as the people of nearby towns, begin construction of a ramp leading up to the top of the hill the city sat on. Now, Alexander's siege equipment could be pushed up to Gaza's wall.

While the catapults and ballistas sent boulders and arrows slamming over the wall, Macedonian soldiers began digging under it. As they opened up space underneath the wall, logs were shoved under to shore it up. Finally, when Alexander and his engineers felt the wall had been weakened enough, the logs were set afire. As they burned away there was nothing left supporting the wall and it began to collapse. A huge section fell away, leaving a gaping opening. The Macedonian and Greek soldiers swarmed into the city. The men of Gaza were killed by the thousands, and the women and children were rounded up to be sold as slaves. After two months, the siege of Gaza was finally over.

ALEXANDER: KING OF EGYPT

There is a story about Gaza that seems to show a streak of cruelty in Alexander. It tells how, after the city was seized, Alexander had Gaza's governor, Batis, brought to him. He began to question Batis, but the man contemptuously ignored him. According to the story, Alexander became so enraged that he had Batis's legs

THE TALE OF ALEXANDER AND THE OMEN

According to one story, as Alexander stood before Gaza making a sacrifice to the gods, a bird dropped a stone on his head. This was the sort of event that people then regarded as an omen. Alexander asked one of his seers to explain the meaning of what had happened.

After thinking about it for a while, the seer told Alexander that he would capture Gaza, but that he should stay out of the fighting for the rest of the day. Alexander stayed back for a while, but when the first assault failed, he insisted on leading the second. As he was rushing forward, a catapult arrow ripped through his shield and armor and tore into his shoulder. It was a serious wound. Most of the soldiers of Alexander's army believed this was what the omen had foretold.

It is true that Alexander was seriously wounded at Gaza, but most historians think this story of the bird was simply made up.

tied to the back of a chariot. He then drove it around and around the city, dragging Batis to his death.

This event is exactly like one in Alexander's favorite epic poem, *The Iliad*. There, the Greek hero Achilles, after killing his Trojan enemy Hector, dragged Hector's body around the walls of Troy behind a chariot. Some historians believe that because Alexander so greatly admired Achilles, who was supposed to have been his ancestor, he was trying to imitate Achilles, and that the story of his treatment of Batis is likely true. Other historians think that the story was simply written by someone who wanted to make Alexander look bad.

With the fall of Gaza, the way into Egypt was now open. Egypt was a vast land of millions of people. In December of 332 B.C., Alexander's army marched in. The Egyptians had no loyalty to Persia and made no attempt to stop Alexander. They did not regard him as a conqueror, but as a liberator, and accepted him as their new king, or "pharaoh." Alexander proceeded to the capital city of Memphis and made the royal palace, a building fit for a King, his home.

THE SON OF A GOD

In late January of 331 B.C., Alexander went by boat to the mouth of the Nile River, where the river empties into the Mediterranean Sea. To Alexander it seemed like a good place for a city, and he decided to build one there and name it after himself—Alexandria. He marked out the position of some of the walls and temples with trails of barley, a type of grain. The work of digging foundations and building walls was done by his soldiers under the direction of Greek architects. Today, Alexandria, Egypt, is the second-largest city in the country and the nation's main port.

In western Egypt, there is an oasis known as Siwa. An oasis is a place in a desert where there is a source of water surrounded by plant life. In Alexander's time, Siwa was considered a sacred place of the god Ammon, and at the temple there, was an oracle. Alexander decided to visit the temple and ask the oracle a question.

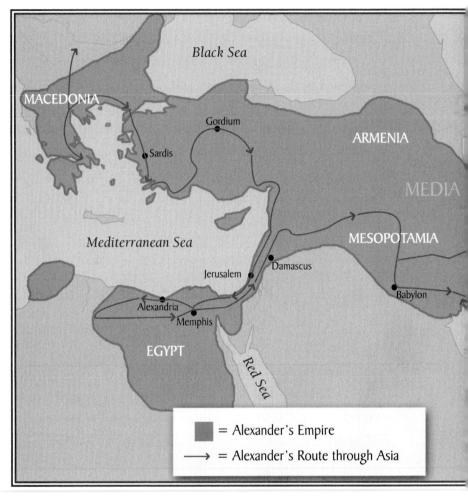

Black Sea

MACEDONIA

Gordium

ARMENIA

Sardis

MEDIA

Mediterranean Sea

MESOPOTAMIA

Jerusalem Damascus

Babylon

Alexandria

Memphis

EGYPT

Red Sea

■ = Alexander's Empire

⟶ = Alexander's Route through Asia

Alexander greatly increased the amount of land in his vast empire.

Reaching the oasis, Alexander walked toward the temple entrance with his commanders behind him. A priest was waiting at the entrance, apparently having been notified of Alexander's arrival. The priest greeted Alexander as "son of Ra," which was later translated to Son of Zeus.[2] It seemed as if the priest was indeed acknowledging that Alexander was the son of a god.

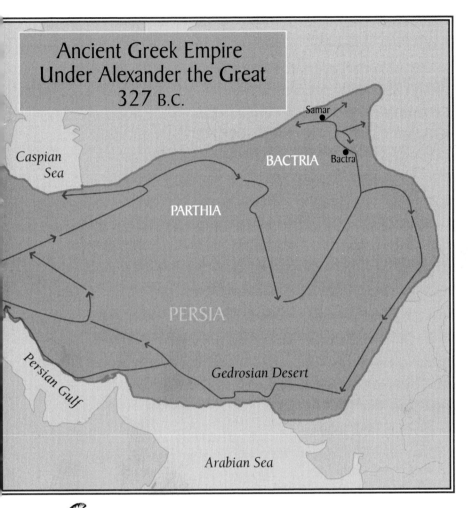

Ancient Greek Empire
Under Alexander the Great
327 B.C.

Samar

Caspian
Sea

BACTRIA   Bactra

PARTHIA

PERSIA

Persian Gulf

Gedrosian Desert

Arabian Sea

THE PERSIAN ARMY AWAITS

Only Alexander was allowed to go into the temple; the others had to wait outside. Therefore, no one heard what Alexander asked the oracle. However, Alexander's Macedonian soldiers apparently believed that Alexander had been told that he was truly the son of the god Zeus, and therefore a god himself.

While Alexander was moving through the Middle East, conquering cities and winning battles, Darius was trying to bribe him. The Persian emperor wanted to make a deal that would leave him with at least part of his empire. He offered huge amounts of land, enormous riches, and one of his daughters to become Alexander's wife, if Alexander would just stop his attempt to conquer all of Persia. There is a story that General Parmenio said that he would accept Darius's offer if he were Alexander. Alexander is said to have replied that he would accept it, too—if he were Parmenio. What he meant was that because he was Alexander, he refused to make any kind of compromise. He sent word back to Darius that he would take everything Darius had offered but would not give anything in return.

Finally, Darius gave up trying to make a deal. He began putting together another enormous army. Alexander learned of this, and in the spring he started marching his army back north along the coast, toward Tyre. At Tyre, he turned and began to move inland, looking for the Persian army.

By July of 331 B.C., it had become apparent that Darius intended to wait for Alexander to meet him in Mesopotamia, which is now the nation of Iraq. Darius was waiting on a broad plain beyond the Tigris River. There were some two hundred thousand foot soldiers and forty-five thousand horsemen in the Persian force.[3] In addition, there were two hundred horse-drawn war chariots with sharp blades attached to their wheels.[4] Any man caught in their path would be slashed to pieces. These chariots had been created especially for fighting Alexander's phalanxes. There were also fifteen huge Indian war elephants, trained to stomp and smash through anything in their way. A driver and two archers sat on each elephant's back.

THE BATTLE BEGINS

Alexander's scouts located Darius's army in late September. Alexander set up his camp seven miles away and gave his soldiers four days of rest. Then, under cover of darkness, he moved the army three miles closer, and put it in battle formation on a hillside overlooking the plain. Most of the next day he spent studying the size, position, and formation of the Persian force.

Alexander's army numbered about forty thousand infantry and seven thousand cavalry.[5] Parmenio and some of the other Macedonian generals were rather concerned that their army was outnumbered. As the sun began to set over the plain, they came to Alexander's tent and urged him to make a night attack that might catch the Persians by surprise. Alexander refused, saying that he would not "steal a victory."[6]

Actually, Darius expected a night attack, and instead of letting his men sleep or relax during the night, he kept them in position with their weapons ready. As a result, when morning came, the Persian troops were sleepy and slow-moving, while the Macedonian men were well rested.

The battle was fought on October 1, 331 B.C. Darius had formed his forces into three columns of foot soldiers with a line of chariots, elephants, and cavalry in front of them, and clusters of cavalry on each side. The Persian line was so long that it would easily be possible for it to curl around each side of Alexander's force and hit the Macedonians from either side or even from the rear. To prevent this, Alexander arranged his army into two lines of infantry mixed with cavalry, one behind the other. If the Persians did try to get around either side of the front line, the rear line could move to that side and meet them head on. With his army in this formation, Alexander moved forward in an attack. Darius sent out hordes of cavalry to charge, and ordered all the chariots forward.

THE CHARGE OF THE CHARIOTS

With a great rumbling that shook the plain, the chariots began to move. As their wheels turned, the sharp blades on them spun in glittering circles. They headed straight for the densely packed Macedonian phalanxes. To deal with them, Alexander sent out hundreds of peltasts.

They dodged around the sides of the chariots hurling javelins at the horses and drivers.

When a horse went down with a javelin in its body, the other horses pulling that same chariot were forced to stop, unable to drag the

Persian war chariots often had blades on their wheels. Archers would ride in the speeding chariots and fire arrows at the enemy.

dead weight. Most of the chariots were stopped this way. Chariots that were not stopped before reaching the front of a Macedonian phalanx were easily dealt with. At a command, the phalanx simply opened up, with men moving to each side so that a broad path was formed in front of the chariot. A chariot could not easily change direction when the horses were galloping at top speed, so it would just have to keep going. Peltasts behind the phalanx would kill the chariot driver with a spear or arrow, and with no one to urge them on, the horses came to a stop. The chariots were all stopped and not one soldier of Alexander's army was killed or hurt by one of them. As for the charging Persian cavalry, Alexander's Macedonian and Thessalian horsemen fought them to a standstill and drove them off.

THE END OF AN EMPIRE

Alexander led his companion cavalry toward the Persian center. Once again, the sight of Alexander coming toward him, sword in hand, was too much for Darius. When his chariot driver went sprawling to the ground with a javelin in his chest, the Persian emperor jumped out of his chariot. He leaped onto the back of a nearby horse and galloped away. At Darius's flight, most of the Persian army fled as well. The battle, which became known as the Battle of Gaugamela, was over. The Persian Empire, which might have been able to conquer Greece, was gone. The art, philosophy, and science developed by Greeks were now free to play a role in the development of the world.

10

AN EMPEROR'S END

Alexander knew he had to lead his army through the entire Persian Empire before he could claim to have conquered it completely. In the weeks after the battle, he marched the army to the cities of Babylon and Susa, in the provinces of Babylonia and Susia, respectively. In both cities, Alexander was greeted with joy by all the citizens, who swore loyalty to him. Knowing it would please the people, he appointed Persians as satraps of the provinces, rather than Macedonians.[1]

Late in December of 331 B.C., Alexander left Susa heading for the city of Persepolis, in the province of Persis. This city had been the capital of the Persian Empire. Not only was it important to strike the final deathblow against Persia by capturing the city that was the home of the emperors, but Persepolis was important for another reason—it contained an enormous treasure. Alexander needed money to pay his mercenary troops and to keep the army equipped and fed, and Persepolis was the answer to his need.

However, Persepolis was not going to greet him peacefully. The city was under the control of a Persian nobleman named Ariobarzanes, who was holding a mountain pass in front of it with an army of forty thousand foot soldiers and seven hundred horsemen. Alexander was afraid that if he simply marched up the main road to the pass, Ariobarzanes would have time to fall back to Persepolis, grab the treasure, and get away. Alexander decided he had to use speed and surprise. He put together a "light" fast-moving force made up of the companion cavalry, light cavalry, Macedonian foot soldiers, and his javelin throwers and archers. They began a quick march through a rugged, difficult mountain region north of the pass. This would enable Alexander to get around behind Ariobarzanes and catch him by surprise.

ALEXANDER RUNS INTO TROUBLE

Alexander had underestimated the Persians. Moving through the rough, mountainous region, the Macedonians suddenly found themselves in a narrow gorge between two sheer cliffs—with a wall built across the end of it! The wall was guarded by Persian soldiers. Obviously, Ariobarzanes had foreseen that someone might try to get behind him and had taken steps to prevent it.

The wall was constructed of stone, but Alexander had his foot soldiers try attacking it. They did their best, trying to scramble to the top hand over hand, using cracks and crevices, but it was hopeless. Persian archers shot arrows down into them, slingers pelted them with missiles, and huge boulders were rolled down on top of them. The casualties were too high, and Alexander ordered the trumpets sounded to call the men back. Was Alexander going to have to give up?

The Macedonians had managed to pull a few Persians off the top of the wall and take them prisoner. Alexander began questioning the prisoners and one of them revealed something that must have made the Macedonian king's heart leap. It was a way of getting past the wall! The man was a slave who had been a shepherd in this area since he was a little boy. He told Alexander that there were hidden paths running up around the cliffs and that men could move on in single file. This was another of those strokes of luck that had helped Alexander before.

A Risky Plan

Alexander offered the prisoner an enormous reward if he would lead the Macedonians up one of the paths. He enthusiastically agreed. Alexander put one of his phalanx commanders, Craterus, in charge of the camp with his phalanx of fifteen hundred hoplites and five hundred cavalry, and told him what to do. He was to stay in place with campfires burning and do what he could to make it look to Ariobarzanes as if an attack might be made at any moment. Meanwhile, Alexander with about fifteen thousand men would go up the path. When they got behind Ariobarzanes's force, and could attack, a trumpet call would be sounded. When he heard it, Craterus was to make a full-scale assault against the wall.

It was a terribly risky plan. For one thing, the prisoner might be leading Alexander's force into a trap. But that night, with the prisoner leading the way, Alexander and his men, each carrying rations for three days, started out on this difficult journey. The soldiers were trying to move as fast as they could, but the path was choked with underbrush and wound up steep slopes. It was now January of 330 B.C., the mountain air was freezing, and there was snow on the ground.

THE PERSIANS ARE SURPRISED

At about midnight they halted for a quick meal of bread and wine. Alexander now made a major decision. He felt it was far more important for some of his men to get to Persepolis and seize the treasure than it was to simply push Ariobarzanes out of the way. Therefore, he split his force, ordering three small phalanxes, about 4,500 men, to head for the distant Arraxes River and build a bridge across it. If Alexander's plan against Ariobarzanes should fail, the phalanxes were to proceed into Persepolis and seize the treasure.

When morning came, Alexander halted his force and waited for night. When darkness closed in, the march resumed, and as the sun began to rise, the Macedonians reached the rear of the Persian camp.

The Persians were caught by surprise, but Ariobarzanes managed to get his force into two lines in front of the camp. Alexander sent all his cavalry around the Persians' right, to turn and strike at that side. He sent his friend Ptolemy with three thousand foot soldiers to hit the Persian left. He led his main force of foot soldiers forward in an attack on the Persian front. Meanwhile, trumpets were blaring to let Craterus, in the Macedonian camp, know that he should charge the wall. Soon, Craterus's men were coming over the wall with no one to stop them, slamming into the Persians from the rear. Hit on all sides, the Persians began fleeing, surrendering, and begging for mercy. The battle was over.

ALEXANDER TAKES PERSEPOLIS

Ariobarzanes managed to retreat with a force of about forty horsemen and a few thousand foot soldiers. He headed for the Arraxes River at a gallop, intent on crossing it and hurrying to Persepolis. Reaching the river, he was probably astounded and horrified to see the three phalanxes Alexander had sent there, formed for battle on the other side. There was no chance of his getting to Persepolis. Alexander, who had seemed to have been stopped dead by the wall in the gorge, had wound up destroying the army that was blocking him, had prevented the Persians from saving their empire's treasure, and was now on the way to securing the treasure for himself.

So, the Macedonian Army marched into the city that had been the center of the Persian Empire. The treasure was located in the great palace of the emperors and was found to be enormous. It has been estimated by present-day experts that it was probably worth hundreds

THE BURNING OF THE PALACE AT PERSEPOLIS

One story about the burning of the great palace at Persepolis says it was done just for fun! An Athenian girl named Thais, who was at a party in the palace with Alexander and his generals, suggested setting the place on fire as a celebration. It was said that Alexander and others snatched up some of the torches used to light the room and ran about setting draperies and wooden furniture ablaze, giggling as they did so.

However, the ruins of the palace were carefully examined by archaeologists in the twentieth century. They found evidence that the fire was very carefully set.[2] Most historians believe that Alexander ordered the palace burned as revenge against the Persians for burning the temples in the city of Athens when they had invaded Greece.

of millions of today's dollars. After most of the treasure was removed, Alexander gave his soldiers permission to loot the palace. Later, he had the beautiful palace burned down.

In Persepolis, Alexander learned that Darius was in the city of Ecbatana, some five hundred miles away, trying to rebuild an army. In May of 330 B.C., Alexander started marching his army toward Ecbatana. Hearing this, Darius retreated eastward, with a force of 6,300 men.

Alexander followed, but some time later learned that Darius was actually being held captive by several

Persian nobles. Alexander sent out groups of cavalry to search the countryside in all directions, looking for Darius and his captors.

Darius Is Murdered

In July of 330 B.C., some Macedonian soldiers finally found Darius in the desert. He had been stabbed with spears and left lying in a cart to die. The Macedonians gave him water, but he died before Alexander arrived. It is said that Alexander was saddened by the way Darius had met his end and spread his own cloak over the former emperor's body. He then had the body sent to Persepolis, to Darius's mother, so that she could have it honorably and properly buried.

With Darius dead, and Alexander in control of most of what had been the Persian Empire, Persia was now "land conquered by the spear." Alexander could claim to be its lawful king. But the Persian nobles who had murdered Darius hoped to make themselves rulers of what remained of the Persian Empire. Most of these men had been satraps of some of the eastern provinces of the Persian Empire. One of them, Bessus, had been satrap of a province known as Bactria, which is now the northern part of Afghanistan. Alexander learned that Bessus was wearing a crown, calling himself "the King of Asia," and raising an army. Alexander could not allow this, of course. He was determined to go after Darius's murderers, wipe them out, and complete his conquest of the entire empire. Accordingly, he led his army through

Though Darius was his enemy, Alexander deeply mourned the loss of the Persian leader. Alexander greatly respected him.

the desert in the direction the Persian nobles and their forces had taken.

PUTTING DOWN A REBELLION

It was midsummer and the desert was broiling under a merciless sun, but Alexander was an example to his men of how to withstand the terrible heat, thirst, hunger, and discomfort of the march. There is a story that when one of his soldiers brought him some water in a helmet, he handed it back to the man, saying, "Why should I drink when you have nothing?"[3]

Alexander learned that Bessus and his accomplices had gone to Bactria. To get to Bactria, Alexander had to pass through some of the other eastern provinces of the empire. The men who had been satraps tried to meet him and let him know that they accepted his rule as King of Asia. In return, Alexander let them keep their positions. This made things easier for Alexander, for he knew that these provinces would be ruled with law and order instead of having different groups fighting for control. He planned to simply let the people of each province he took over keep on living as they had, with the same laws and customs they were used to.

However, one of those satraps who had kept his position turned out to be a bad choice. He was Satibarzanes, who had been governor of the province of Hariva. Satibarzanes was one of the men who had murdered Darius, and he had close ties to Bessus. He now put together a force of troops and declared that he was in rebellion against Alexander.

This was a dangerous situation for the Macedonian Army and Alexander moved at once to put an end to it. He took the companion cavalry, a force of light cavalry, some archers and light infantry, and two four-thousand-man phalanxes, and turned back toward Hariva. Hearing he was coming, Satibarzanes fled with two thousand horsemen. The Harivan troops left behind tried to put up a fight, but were worn down over several weeks. Their leaders were executed and the foot soldiers sold into slavery. Alexander pardoned the ordinary citizens of any wrongdoing.

PURSUING THE ENEMY

In August, Alexander's army marched into a part of Afghanistan that is today known as "The Desert of Death."[1] At that time of year, this part of Afghanistan is swept by heavy winds that whip the sand and dust into quick-moving clouds. Arriving at the town of Phrada, Alexander halted the march and ordered a nine-day rest. The soldiers pegged their tents down to make places of shelter from the dust-filled wind.

Something shocking and completely unexpected now took place. One of the royal pages brought a boy to see Alexander—he had learned of a plot to have Alexander killed.

One of the most troubling things for Alexander was that the plot apparently involved one of his top officers, Philotas. Philotas was the commander of the companion cavalry and the son of the loyal old general Parmenio!

Alexander called together his councilors. They all agreed that Philotas should be put on trial. This was done by calling Philotas, and those accused of plotting with him, before the six thousand Macedonian soldiers who formed part of the army. One of the accused men, a Macedonian soldier named Dimnus, killed himself rather than stand trial. He probably feared being tortured, which was the common way of getting information.

Philotas was tortured by Hephaestion and some of Alexander's other friends, and finally admitted that he had known of the plot and not warned Alexander about it. He and the others were found guilty. They were executed by having javelins hurled into their bodies by Macedonian soldiers.

THE MURDER OF PARMENIO

This was not the end of Alexander's efforts to deal with the plot. Philotas's father, Parmenio, was back in Ecbatana, in command of nearly twelve thousand Macedonian and Greek soldiers.

Could Parmenio have been involved in the plot against Alexander? Parmenio was well-liked by his soldiers. If he rebelled against Alexander, he had enough troops to cause Alexander's army trouble.

A Macedonian law required that any male relative of a man executed for treason against the king was also to be executed. Alexander ordered Parmenio's death. He sent a trusted officer back to Ecbatana with an order for Parmenio's execution. Parmenio was caught by surprise in a garden and stabbed to death. He had served both Philip and Alexander faithfully for almost thirty years. He was more than seventy years old.

Why would there have been a plot to kill Alexander? Many historians have tried to figure this out. The most common belief is that many Macedonians in the army were annoyed that Alexander was allowing Persians to stay in control of their provinces instead of appointing Macedonians as governors. Some soldiers and officers, both Macedonians and Greeks, may have felt that Alexander was being too kind to people who had twice tried to conquer Greece. They may have felt that if Alexander were assassinated, and another Macedonian became king, then Macedonians and Greeks would gain more profit from the conquest of Persia.

A MARCH OVER THE MOUNTAINS

Immediately after the murder of Parmenio, the troops under his command in Ecbatana were ordered to march to join Alexander. They finally arrived, after the long march, in December of 330 B.C. In early spring of 329 B.C., Alexander made sacrifices, was assured that the omens were good, and resumed the march into Bactria to pursue Bessus. To get into Bactria, his army had to cross the mountains known today as the Hindu Kush, which form part of the boundary between Afghanistan and Pakistan. The snow on the mountain heights had not begun to melt and Bessus would never dream that Alexander would try crossing the mountains under such conditions.

Including the troops from Ecbatana, the army numbered about forty thousand men. It was a huge column, stretching out for miles, tramping up into the mountains. As the army moved higher, the cold grew more intense and the snow was deeper. Men were blinded by the glare of the sun on the whiteness all around them, and lost fingers and toes to frostbite. Food was scarce. As the bundles of food carried by the packhorses and mules were used up, the soldiers began to slaughter the animals for food. There were no trees for firewood among the crags and boulders, so the animals were eaten raw. Men were sometimes able to catch trout in mountain streams, and these, too, were eaten raw. Just as Alexander had shown courage and endurance leading his men through the desert, he now used courage and endurance to lead them over the mountain. He marched on foot, as his men were doing, and often stopped to help up a man who had slipped in the snow.

There were several passes leading through the mountains, and Alexander chose one called the Khawak Pass. Once the army began to move downhill, conditions improved. Farther down, there were communities of people living in snug huts blanketed with the snow. They had extra food to sell to the army. It had taken the immense force sixteen days to cross the mountains.

THE PURSUIT OF BESSUS

Alexander's army came down out of the mountains in terrible shape. If Bessus had attacked right then, he might have ended Alexander's conquests and rebuilt the Persian Empire with himself as emperor. But once again Alexander had outsmarted his enemy. Bessus was apparently astounded that Alexander had appeared so quickly. He and his friends lost their nerve and headed for the Oxus River, where they crossed over into the region that is now part of the Republic of Uzbekistan. Before leaving, they destroyed all the boats they did not need, in hope of preventing Alexander from following.

Now that Alexander's army was out of the mountains, in a region of plentiful food and supplies, its condition began to improve. The horses that had died or been killed for food were replaced. Men who had died or been badly injured were replaced by Persian and Mede soldiers who now regarded Alexander as their ruler. Alexander discharged his oldest Macedonian and Thessalian soldiers, who had been with him since the crossing of the Hellespont and sent them home. Now that he was in Bactria, and about to follow Bessus into the northernmost province, Sogdiana, Alexander believed that his work of conquering the Persian Empire was nearly over.

It was midsummer when Alexander began the pursuit of Bessus. The army marched at night because of the terrible heat during daytime. Reaching the banks of the Oxus, Alexander set his men to prepare for the crossing by making rafts and floats, as they had done when they crossed the Danube. It took five days to make the crossing. On the other side of the river, Alexander received a message from two Persian nobles who were with Bessus. These men, Spitamenes and Dataphernes, informed Alexander that they were holding Bessus prisoner and were willing to turn him over. They were probably hoping to make some sort of deal with

Alexander, to get him to spare their lives if they gave him Bessus.

Alexander sent Ptolemy and a cavalry force to look for Bessus and his captors. They found Bessus, abandoned and in chains, in a small village and brought him back to Alexander. Alexander apparently thought he deserved serious punishment for the murder of Darius, and had him whipped until he was nearly dead.[2] Bessus was then sent to the Persian that Alexander had appointed governor of Bactria, who subjected him to the Persian punishment of having his nose and ears cut off. Finally, Bessus was sent to Ecbatana where he was executed.

As he battled through the Persian Empire, Alexander visited an ancient city near the present-day city of Alinda, Turkey. These ruins are all that remain of the ancient city.

Sogdiana Refuses to Surrender

Alexander now took over the Sogdian city of Samarkand, the main fortress of Cyropolis, and seven smaller forts that guarded the northeastern frontier—all to be used as bases. He put a small number of troops in each. Confident that Bactria and Sogdiana were ready to acknowledge him as King of Asia, he sent out messages requesting the Bactrian and Sogdian nobles to come to him.

However, he was mistaken in thinking the two provinces had given up. When Spitamenes received Alexander's summons, he believed that Alexander probably meant to make him prisoner. He formed an army and attacked Alexander's bases at Cyropolis and the seven small forts. They were quickly captured, the Macedonian troops Alexander had left in them were wiped out, and Spitamenes left Sogdian troops in charge. Alexander realized that Sogdiana was in full revolt.

As usual, Alexander acted at once. Of course, he had to recapture his bases rapidly, but he knew that if the Sogdian troops in them learned he was coming to attack them, they would probably all leave the forts and join together to form an army. He had to prevent this. He sent Craterus and a fifteen-hundred-man phalanx to Cyropolis to surround it, pinning the Sogdians inside. He sent his two companion cavalry units to the two northernmost forts to keep an eye on them from a distance. The cavalry commanders were ordered to attack any Sogdians who tried to leave. He took the rest of his troops to the three nearest forts and proceeded to take them by storm, one after another, within forty-eight hours. He set fire to one of the forts, sending a cloud of smoke into the sky. This would make the Sogdians in the two northern forts aware that Alexander's forces were on the attack and probably heading toward them. As Alexander had guessed, the Sogdians in the two forts quickly tried to leave. They ran into the hidden cavalry, which charged into them and wiped them out.

ALEXANDER FINDS A WAY INTO CYROPOLIS

This left the main fortress of Cyropolis with its Sogdians trapped inside, but ready to fight to the death to keep Alexander out. He did not want a long fight and he did not want to use up a lot of his troops, so he studied the place carefully, looking for an easy way in.

A river flowed through the fortress, and Alexander noticed that at this time of year it was nearly dry and so shallow that men could walk in it. The river entered the fortress through a tunnel that had its opening in one of the walls. As night fell, Alexander had men start slamming at the fortress's main gate with battering rams, to draw the attention of the Sogdians. Then, Alexander and a force of archers, slingers, and hypaspists quietly sneaked to the tunnel entrance and crept into it. Moving through the tunnel, they came out inside the fortress, attacked the Sogdians from the rear, and managed to get one of the smaller gates open, which let the rest of the army in. A vicious battle took place in which some eight thousand Sogdians were killed and seven thousand surrendered. Alexander suffered a nasty head wound

ALEXANDER'S CITIES

One of the ancient writers said that Alexander had seventy cities built in Asia.[3] Apparently, about thirty were named Alexandria and the others had other names. Some were actually just small forts that Alexander built for use as military bases, but many were cities of thousands of people. The buildings were constructed of bricks, made from mud and straw, dried hard in the hot sun.

Alexander was not simply trying to preserve his name or "show off." The cities all had a purpose. For one thing, they provided homes for Alexander's veteran soldiers who had become too old or too crippled from wounds to be able to fight any longer. Many of these men had Persian wives and children. Persian people from the surrounding countryside were also invited to settle in the cities, if they wished. Everyone was allowed to keep their own religion and customs, although the Persians were encouraged to speak Greek and to learn about Greek and Macedonian customs. Thus, Alexander was accomplishing one of his goals, to mix together the different people of his empire to make them into one.

Many of Alexander's cities no longer exist today, but a few are still standing in various parts of the Middle East, having been rebuilt many times over the centuries.

when he was struck by a sling stone. He was knocked unconscious; when he came to, he could not see or talk for a time.

A few days later, the remaining two forts were easily taken, and Alexander had his bases back. Once again he had used foresight, careful observation, and another stroke of luck—the shallowness of the river—to gain his victory.

ALEXANDER BUILDS A CITY AND ENCOUNTERS THE SCYTHIANS

Now, Alexander had his soldiers begin building a walled city on the Jaxartes River. It was to be used as an advanced base. He called it Alexandria the Farthest, as it was the farthest of all the cities named Alexandria that he ordered built in Asia. It still stands, now named Khodzent, in the nation of Tajikistan.

There was a problem with Alexander's plans, however. The Jaxartes marked the border of Sogdiana, and beyond it lay the lands of a nomadic people known as the Scythians. The Scythian warriors were all "light" cavalrymen who wore no helmets or armor, and many did not even carry shields. Their main weapons were bows that could shoot arrows about eighty yards. They were superb horsemen and deadly archers, well-known to be fierce fighters. They had heard of Alexander's conquests and the city he was building, and were now gathering on the banks of the Jaxartes to prevent him from crossing the river into their country. Alexander knew that unless he crushed Spitamenes's rebellion quickly, a Scythian army might well come into Sogdiana and join the Sogdians against him.

12

THE
SCYTHIANS
AND BEYOND

Alexander decided he had to turn his full attention to the Scythians. They continued to gather near the Jaxartes River, and soon had a sizable army. Every day they yelled insults at the Greek and Macedonian soldiers across from them, daring Alexander to try to invade their country. Alexander could not ignore them, because if he left the river to march against Spitamenes and the other rebellious forces in Sogdiana and Bactria, the Scythians would surely cross the river and be at his rear. He had to do something to make them afraid of trying such a thing. He told his officers that they could not let the Scythians continue to insult them without punishment. "Our role is to attack," he insisted. "The day on which we put ourselves on the defensive will see us lost!"[1] He felt he had to invade the Scythians' land, get them into a battle, and beat them so soundly they would be afraid of him forevermore.

THE ASSAULT ON THE SCYTHIANS

To invade Scythia, Alexander's army would have to cross the Jaxartes. But to try crossing a river against an army in which every soldier was a dead-on shot with a bow and arrow could mean enormously high casualties. Once again, Alexander had to think up a special way of doing it.

Alexander knew his catapults and ballistas could all shoot missiles farther than the Scythians could shoot arrows with their bows. He lined up all his missile-throwing machines along the riverbank and put his soldiers to work constructing some twelve thousand rafts. When everything was ready, the assault began.

Along the riverbank, the rafts slid out into the river. With thumps and creaks the war machines began throwing boulders and giant spears across the water. The Scythians had ridden down to the very edge of the bank on their side, intending to send a storm of arrows into the rafts. But, instead, a storm of war machine missiles came hurtling into them! Men were knocked off their horses with smashed bodies and broken bones. Others were pierced by spears as thick as a man's arm that went right through them. The Scythians turned and rode back out of range of this deadly barrage.

ALEXANDER DISPLAYS A NEW KIND OF WARFARE

At the front of each raft in the first line of oncoming rafts crouched several soldiers with big hoplite shields locked together. In this way, Alexander had turned the rafts into armored vessels!

As the rafts got close enough for Scythian arrows to reach them, the shields protected the men, mostly archers and slingers, crouched on the rafts. As the rafts bumped the riverbank, Alexander's men sprang out. They spread out, and moving forward, began pouring arrows and missiles into the Scythian horsemen.

Behind them came Alexander's cavalry, the horses swimming and the men on rafts and floats. Reaching the bank, the men quickly mounted. Led by Alexander, they moved forward behind the archers and slingers. Suddenly, Alexander swung a portion of the companion cavalry and his javelin-throwing light cavalry around the archers and slingers and slammed into the Scythian horsemen from the side. The Scythians had no time to use their bows, no weapon to counter the long stabbing spears of the armored companion cavalry, and no armor or shields to protect them from the savagely hurled javelins. By the hundreds, men were falling from their horses. Other men were turning their horses and galloping away. The Scythian army was in flight.

THE SCYTHIANS SEEK PEACE

It was a terribly hot day, and at some point during the battle Alexander had gulped down a drink of what turned out to be polluted water. He became violently sick and was unable to lead his men in pursuit of the fleeing Scythians. About one thousand Scythians had been killed and 150 captured, so this was not the major victory Alexander had hoped for. However, it apparently was enough to impress the Scythian leaders. Alexander had shown them that he could come up with methods of beating their way of warfare. Within days they sent emissaries to ask for peace and an alliance, which he quickly agreed to. He had done exactly what he had hoped for, which was to make sure the Scythians would never dare cross the river and join his enemies in Sogdiana and Bactria.

In this battle against the Scythians, Alexander had done another new thing in warfare. Years before, when fighting in Illyria, he had used artillery—missile-throwing weapons—to protect the withdrawal of his army across a river. Here, he had used artillery to protect the *advance* of his army across a river. This was the first time in history this was done.[2]

In the early spring of 328 B.C., the Bactrian and Sogdian rebels began making hit-and-run raids throughout the two provinces. To combat this, Alexander split his army into a number of forces that could move fast and hit hard. One of these forces, led by Alexander's general Coenus, fought a group of rebels led by Spitamenes, and defeated them badly. Spitamenes lost eight hundred men, while Coenus's losses were thirty-seven. The rebels decided Spitamenes was no longer a worthy leader. They murdered him and sent his head to Alexander, hoping that would keep Alexander from coming after them!

THE MURDER OF CLEITUS

In the autumn, Alexander went to Samarkand for what might be called a short vacation from constant warfare. At this time, when he was not on the march with the army, his days were leisurely.

Upon getting up in the morning, he first made a sacrifice to the gods and then sat down to breakfast. After that, he often spent the day hunting, something he loved to do. He would even hunt just birds or foxes, if there was nothing else. On some days, however, he worked, holding trials of soldiers who had committed crimes or avoided their duty, or taking care of the needs of the army. At times, he simply read for hours, which he found very enjoyable. In the late afternoon, he would often check with his cooks and bakers about the evening meal. He would have his meal fairly late at night with his commanders, reclining on a couch, as was the Greek and Macedonian way.

For some time, Alexander had been acting more and more like an Asian ruler, such as Darius had been. He often dressed in Persian clothing rather than Macedonian. He allowed the Persians who had become his followers to treat him with Asian forms of respect, such as deep bows. This was not a Greek or Macedonian custom, and it angered and disturbed most of the Macedonians and Greeks of his army. Alexander was also drinking a great deal more wine than he ever had before. He was showing signs of flying into quick rages. All this led to a terrible tragedy. While dining together one night, Alexander's old and good friend Cleitus, who had once saved his life, got drunk and began to tease and criticize Alexander for acting like a Persian instead of a Macedonian.

Alexander, too, was drunk. Both men became angry. Cleitus apparently shouted that Alexander owed his victories to the army his father, Philip, had created and trained. "All your glory is due to your father," Cleitus told Alexander.[3] This so enraged Alexander that he grabbed a spear and drove it into Cleitus's chest, killing him.

Immediately, Alexander seemed horrified by what he had done. He tried to shove the bloody spear point into his own chest, but his bodyguards leaped forward and prevented him. They carried him off to his bed.

For a time, he spent his days in bed, refusing to eat. Then, some of his councilors came to talk to him. The seer Aristander told him that he might have angered a god, who had punished him by making him kill Cleitus. Thus, the murder was not his fault, Aristander insisted. The philosopher Anexagorus told him that it was not his fault because he was a king, and a king just could not do anything wrong! Eventually, Alexander began to eat and become himself again.

"SOLDIERS WITH WINGS"

The revolt against Alexander in Bactria and Sogdiana was still swirling. It was now led by two nobles named Oxyartes and Chorienes. Before Alexander could lay full claim to having conquered the Persian Empire, he had to complete the conquest of these last two provinces. He set out to do just that in the winter of 327 B.C.

Oxyartes, his family, and his soldiers were holed up in a fortress built on a huge rock, called the Sogdian Rock, sticking out of a mountainside. Alexander headed there first. There was a cliff behind the fortress, and if soldiers could reach the cliff top they could easily get into the fortress. However, the sides of the cliff were sheer, straight up and down, and a fall would be certain death. It seemed impossible that any man could scale the cliff. When Alexander stood at the foot of the Sogdian Rock and called upon the people in the fortress to surrender, they merely laughed. Taunting him, they said they were only afraid of soldiers with wings.

This was the sort of challenge that Alexander could not ignore. Many of the men in his army had been born and reared in the mountains of Macedonia and had done mountain climbing. Alexander offered enormous amounts of money to any men who could make it to the cliff top. Three hundred men volunteered. In the dark of night, hammering iron tent pegs into the thick ice of the cliff they pulled themselves up hand over hand. Thirty did fall to their deaths, but the rest reached the top. When Alexander called on the people in the fortress to look at his "winged soldiers," they were astounded, and fearful. It seemed to them as if Alexander had done something supernatural.[4] When he promised good treatment if they surrendered, they agreed.

⚔ ALEXANDER MEETS ROXANA AND AVOIDS ASSASSINATION

One of the captives under the surrender was Oxyartes's daughter, Roxana, who was said to be the most beautiful woman in the Persian Empire. Apparently, Alexander instantly fell in love with her. Within a few months, she became his wife. Alexander appointed her father one of his councilors.

The last rebel leader, Chorienes, was also in a fortress, known as the Rock of Chorienes. Alexander sent Oxyartes to talk to Chorienes, who agreed to surrender. Alexander appointed him governor of Sogdiana.

In the spring of 327 B.C., Alexander called all his forces together at the city of Bactra, in Bactria. He seemed to be taking a short vacation from warfare. He and his officers held parties, gave feasts, and went on hunts.

During one hunt, a royal page broke a rule. He was punished by being beaten and having his horse taken away. Burning with anger and humiliation, the young man convinced five other pages to join him in a plot to kill Alexander. However, another page learned of the plot and reported it to General Ptolemy, who at once told Alexander about it. The five pages in the plot were seized and tortured until they admitted their guilt. They were all executed, along with a number of men who were known to be friendly with them.

Alexander then began planning his next major campaign—the invasion of India.

INVADING INDIA

Alexander began making his plans to invade India in late 327 B.C. No Macedonian or Greek had ever been to India, so Alexander had no idea how huge India actually was. He also did not know that beyond it there was another vast empire—China. Alexander believed that India extended a short distance eastward to an ocean, and that it was the last portion of Asia. Therefore, he felt he had to conquer it in order to fulfill his vow to become king of Asia.

In the late winter of 327 B.C., Alexander and his army set out. The army numbered about seventy-five thousand men from all parts of the former Persian Empire, as well as Macedonians and Greeks. All these men were treated equally, for this was now an army of Alexander's empire. Alexander was achieving one of his goals of bringing Macedonians, Greeks, and Asians together under his leadership.

The army traveled with engineers (specialists in building roads, bridges, and other structures), scientists, seers, record keepers, cattle herders, cooks, doctors, soldiers' wives and children, and even teachers for the children![1] Alexander split the group in two, sending half straight ahead, under Hephaestion and Perdiccas, to build a bridge across the Indus River, which was regarded as the border of India. He took the other half on a route that protected Hephaestion and Perdiccas's flank against barbarian tribes.

The army Alexander led met resistance at once. Most of the tribes lived in fortified villages that they generally defended fiercely. These places often had to be taken by storm, using siege weapons to batter down walls or gates and then charging in. In the very first such battle, Alexander was wounded by an arrow that lanced his shoulder. Months later, in another battle for a walled city, he was wounded by an arrow that went into his leg.

A FACE-OFF AT THE HYDASPES RIVER

After capturing or accepting the surrender of most places that might have caused trouble, Alexander had his army build a number of boats. On these, the army floated down the Indus River to where the other half of the army had built a bridge. It was in early spring of 326 B.C. that Alexander's entire force crossed the Indus. The region Alexander invaded is now part of the nation of Pakistan, which was once the western part of India.

Moving into this new land, the Greeks and Macedonians began to see strange new kinds of plants and animals. Alexander was probably as excited as any of the scientists traveling with the army. It was said that

Alexander regarded knowledge of new plants and animals as one of the rewards of victory.[2]

A number of tribes lived in the land across the Indus. Most of the rulers of these tribes came to meet Alexander, saying they accepted him as king of Asia. Some even brought him troops to aid his army. The rulers were happy to be on Alexander's side, because they were fearful of a powerful kingdom that lay beyond the Hydaspes River, some two hundred miles from the Indus. They were hoping Alexander could conquer it.

The Indians wore clothing made of linen cloth that covered them down to their feet. On their heads were turbans, and many of them wore earrings. The men all had bushy beards, which they never shaved.

The Greeks and Macedonians discovered that the Indians had wise men like the philosophers of Greece. They studied the stars, and it was said that they could foretell the future. But the soldiers did not care for their appearance. These men had wild, bushy hair and beards. Some of them were naked. In general, the Macedonians and Greeks tended to look down on the Indians.

Alexander sent messengers to the king of the region beyond the Hydaspes River, a man named Porus, to come and meet with him and swear submission to him as king of Asia. Porus sent back word that he would meet Alexander at the Hydaspes—with an army. Alexander started marching his troops to the river. Reaching the Hydaspes, now called the Jhelum, Alexander saw that Porus had placed his army on the far bank of the river so that Alexander would have to cross to get to him.

Porus's army consisted of about thirty thousand foot soldiers, four thousand horsemen, three hundred chariots, and two hundred war elephants.[3] The foot soldiers were mostly archers, armed with bows, as long as the men were tall, that shot three-foot-long arrows. Porus had put a strong force at every place along the river where Alexander might try to cross.

ALEXANDER PLANS A TRICK

It was obvious to Alexander that simply trying to push across the river by force would be a disaster. Springtime was the rainy season in this part of India, and days of heavy rain had made the river high and fast moving. It was a half-mile wide in most places. The soldiers would have to wade slowly across in deep, rushing water. The Indian soldiers would be able to shoot arrows into them, and by the time the survivors got to the other side, many war elephants would have been waiting for them. Most elephants had a crew of a driver and two archers or spearmen that sat on the animal's back. The elephants were protected by leather armor and their tusks were capped with sharp metal points. These were creatures that the Macedonians and Greeks had seen before, at the Battle of Gaugamela, but had never actually fought against. Now, they would almost certainly have to fight them and were rather concerned about being stomped to death by the charging beasts.

Alexander had to find a way of getting his troops to the other side quickly, without the Indians seeing them coming. He had to use surprise. This would require a careful plan using deception and trickery.

Alexander began by trying to give Porus a feeling of false security. He made it look as if he were simply putting his army into a large encampment on his side of the river, right across from Porus's camp. He made announcements to his troops that he intended to wait until the end of the rainy season before doing anything, and he had huge amounts of supplies collected from the surrounding countryside, as if he were stocking up for the months ahead.

He knew word of all this would be carried to Porus by spies. Hopefully, Porus would believe there would be nothing to worry about for a few months.

If Alexander's soldiers were not careful, Porus's war elephants could crush them.

ALEXANDER KEEPS PORUS GUESSING

However, Alexander quickly began doing things to make Porus and the Indians uncertain about his intentions. At night, he began making what seemed to be attempted crossings all along the river. Porus's troops on the other side suddenly saw moving figures and flaring torches and heard shouts and trumpet calls. Alexander was actually using only small amounts of troops, but it was hard to tell this in the darkness. Porus's soldiers hustled into position, prepared to fight off a determined advance— but then, nothing would happen. Night after night, and often in daytime as well, faked crossings were made at different places along the river. The men of Porus's army were kept busy running from place to place.

Meanwhile, Alexander was scouting all along the river, looking for the place where the crossing could actually be made. Eventually, he found it, about eighteen miles up the river from his camp. It was what is called a headland, a section of high land sticking some distance out into the river. It was wide enough to hold several thousand troops and it was heavily forested, so the troops could gather among the trees without being seen from the other side. Better still, there was a small heavily wooded island in the river right in front of the headland. This would help block the view even more.

The boats that the army had used to cross the Indus River had been left about a hundred miles behind, under guard, and Alexander now sent for them. They were brought in wagons, traveling only at night for secrecy. Some were taken to the headland where they were hidden among the trees; others were taken to the main camp and concealed in tents. When this was done, Alexander stationed observers all along the riverbank from the headland to the camp, to watch Porus's troops.

ALEXANDER STRIKES!

Alexander kept faking crossings at night for several weeks, and Porus kept his soldiers and elephants moving back and forth just in case one of the fake crossings was a real one. But Alexander's observers could see that the Indian troops were getting careless. They had reached a point where they felt that Alexander was merely fooling them all the time and that the Macedonian king did not really intend to try to cross the river. They paid less and less attention to the fake crossings. When Alexander decided they had grown careless enough, he struck!

It was late May, still the rainy season, and he picked a dark, wild night, with a noisy thunderstorm raging. Under cover of this noise and darkness, ten thousand Macedonian foot soldiers and five thousand horsemen marched out of camp toward the headland, where the boats and rafts were being pulled out of hiding. The soldiers moved as silently as possible, well back from the river, behind the trees. Meanwhile, another five thousand foot soldiers and a thousand horsemen moved silently down to the riverbank and took positions all along the river. This was a precaution Alexander had thought of. If Porus should decide to bring a force across the river and make an attack, which would be a good surprise move, Alexander wanted enough men on hand to fight him off.

At Alexander's camp, making plenty of noise with torches flaring, eight thousand foot soldiers and about three thousand cavalrymen were getting into formation. Alexander had one of his officers who resembled him dress in his armor and helmet and direct everything. Anyone watching from across the river, in Porus's camp, would think it was Alexander, getting his troops ready to make a crossing. However, this force, which was under the command of Craterus, had orders not to cross the river unless they saw Porus moving troops and elephants out of his camp.

THE MOVE ACROSS THE RIVER

Alexander's attacking force began to move across the river to the accompaniment of deafening rumbles of thunder that helped cover up the sounds of the crossing. His foot soldiers crossed in the boats and his horses swam across with their riders moving alongside them on floats made of animal skins. Within hours, Alexander was on the other side of the river with some six thousand foot soldiers and five thousand horsemen. He immediately began to move toward Porus's camp.

When informed that troops were moving toward him, Porus was confused and uncertain. He could see what he believed to be Alexander's main force in the camp across the river, apparently getting ready to make a crossing. But then what had just come across the river?

Was it Alexander's actual main force or was it what soldiers call a diversionary force—a small number of troops sent to lure the enemy into leaving their position?

Porus decided it must be a diversionary force and sent a small force of only 2,000 horsemen and 120 chariots to deal with it.

This was exactly what Alexander had planned for. His five thousand Macedonian and Thessalian cavalry not only outnumbered the Indians but also had the skill and battle experience to outfight them. Porus's force was totally wiped out.

ALEXANDER'S GREATEST VICTORY

Porus decided to fight a defensive battle and moved quickly, putting his elephants in a long line, 100 feet apart, with 30,000 foot soldiers behind them and 150 chariots and 2,000 horsemen on each side. Alexander had formed his foot soldiers into a huge phalanx and now moved it and a large force of cavalry toward the left side of the line. To counter this, Porus moved the cavalry from his right side to his left. However, Alexander had sent a cavalry force around to the rear, and that force and his now had Porus's cavalry trapped between them. Charges into their front and rear wiped them out. The chariots were helpless against the cavalry, and with its bristling spears the phalanx forced the elephants to back up into the troops behind them, who turned and fled. Porus's army began to dissolve.

Seeing what was happening, Craterus brought his force at the camp across the river and went after Porus's fleeing forces, which had about twelve thousand men killed and nine thousand captured.[4] Porus, mounted on an elephant, tried to keep fighting, although wounded and covered with blood. Eventually, listening to the pleas of the men still with him, he surrendered.

Alexander had seen that Porus had fought bravely, and admired him for it. The two men became good friends. After Porus swore his loyalty, Alexander gave him back his kingdom and even added more lands to it.

Although he may not have been aware of it, this was Alexander's greatest victory. To this day, the Battle of the Hydaspes River is studied at military colleges such as West Point as the best example of the method an army can use to cross a river that is held by an enemy force.

A Sad Loss

Despite his victory, Alexander suffered a sad personal loss. His horse, Bucephalus, which had been his steed for some eighteen years, had died on the battlefield. Alexander ordered a city named Bucephala to be built on the riverbank. The city no longer exists today.

Alexander let the army rest for a time in Porus's kingdom, where food was plentiful. Trees were also plentiful, and Alexander had many cut down and sawed into planks. His soldiers began to build a fleet of ships. Alexander believed that with his victory on the Hydaspes he was now truly king of Asia. He felt that the only thing he should now do was to march to "the end of India" and see where it projected into the ocean. However, he soon began to realize that India, and Asia, was far bigger than he had thought. He also realized that he might have to fight his way through it! There were rumors of distant kings with enormous armies.

THE DEATH
OF A GOD

Alexander put the army on the march again, in a northeasterly direction. The army reached the banks of the Hyphasis River (now the Beas), which would have to be crossed to continue marching eastward. But the Macedonian and Greek soldiers did not welcome the idea of trying to conquer an enormous, unknown country. They had been fighting for years and just wanted to go home. Alexander was aware of this, and called a meeting of all the army's officers. He probably thought he could talk the officers into continuing on, but they indicated that the army was not willing. They had appointed one of Alexander's best and most trusted generals, Coenus, to be their spokesman. "Do not be a leader of unwilling troops,"[1] he advised Alexander, and told him he would never find the old spirit and courage in the men if they were unwilling.

Alexander became furious. It is recorded that he announced that he would go on by himself and would not make any Macedonian go with him who did not want to. He angrily shouted that those who wished to go home could do so, and they should "tell their friends that they had come back leaving their king surrounded by foes!"[2] Then he turned and strode into his tent.

He stayed there for three days. His soldiers did not send any word to him that they had changed their minds. Finally, he came out of the tent and asked the seers to find out if the gods promised good luck if the river was crossed. This was done by killing a goat and examining its intestines. The seers told Alexander that the gods were sending word not to cross the river. Reluctantly, Alexander told the army that he agreed to turn back and head for home. The men began to shout and cheer.

The Army Starts for Home

It was now the end of August. The monotonous rain had finally ended and the land was drying. Alexander conducted ceremonies to honor the gods, then started the army marching back toward the heart of Porus's country. Reaching the Hydaspes River, where he had fought the great battle against Porus, he sent an order for the fleet of eighty ships that had been built to come to him. Reinforcements had come from Persia, and he also ordered them to join him. His army now numbered about one hundred twenty thousand men.

Alexander had decided to head back to Persia by having the fleet sail down the Hydaspes and Indus rivers to the Arabian Sea, with the army moving alongside on land. In early November of 326 B.C., a trumpet sounded and a portion of the army began moving onto the ships. A force of some forty to fifty thousand troops formed up on each side of the river, one commanded by Craterus, the other by Hephaestion. Another trumpet call sounded, and a great roar began, as 2,400 oars started to creak and the steps of thousands of men and horses thudded into the ground.

Both the army and the ships were heading into territory of many different tribes. Most of these, having heard of Alexander's victories, agreed to accept Alexander as king and let him pass through their lands without any trouble. However, Alexander learned that two tribes, the Mahlavas and Ksudrakas, intended to join forces and fight him. They were powerful tribes that together could oppose him with an army of ninety thousand foot soldiers, ten thousand horsemen, and nine hundred chariots. This was nearly as strong a force as his.

An Assault From the Desert

Alexander knew his best move was to attack one of the tribes before it combined its forces with the other. He launched a whirlwind campaign against the Mahlavas. He sent two forces to places where they could block Ksudrakas troops from coming into Mahlavas territory in order to help the Mahlavas. He sent the fleet up a river that flowed through Mahlavas country, with an army moving alongside it on land. The Mahlavas would think this was the main force coming to attack them. But, as usual, Alexander had carefully scouted the region and found the perfect place where the main attack could come from. It was a bleak desert, fiercely hot and nearly waterless, and the Mahlavas would never expect an army to come out of it. When that army with Alexander at its head suddenly appeared, moving toward the first Mahlavas city in its path, the city's defenders were caught totally by surprise. Those camped around the city were wiped out. Two thousand more were killed when Alexander's troops broke into the city after two assaults.

Alexander led his army deeper into Mahlavas territory. He came upon a small Mahlavas force crossing a river into Ksudrakas territory and instantly attacked, killing many and capturing others.

Some tribesmen managed to escape from both these battles, and news of Alexander's victories began to spread. The main Mahlavas army, fifty thousand strong, began moving toward Ksudrakas territory, to join forces with their ally. Alexander caught up to them with his cavalry, and although greatly outnumbered, managed to pin them down until his foot soldiers arrived. At the sight of the phalanx moving toward them, the Mahlavas retreated to a nearby walled city and shut themselves up inside it. It was the city of Multan.

THE TRIBES GIVE UP

Alexander, of course, determined to take the city by storm. As his soldiers began placing ladders against the walls, Alexander nimbly sped up the nearest ladder and leaped over the top of the wall, becoming the first Macedonian into the city. It was now that he took the terrible arrow wound in his lung that nearly killed him and led his soldiers to believe he was dead. The city was taken, and most of those within it were slaughtered.

As Alexander was recovering, emissaries began to come to him from the Mahlavas, the Ksudrakas, and a number of other nearby tribes. These people had decided that they simply could not defeat Alexander. They brought gifts and treasure, pleaded to be allowed to surrender, and agreed to accept him as their king.

The army and the fleet continued southward until they reached the Indus River. All along the way, more tribes surrendered. Word of Alexander's power traveled ahead of him, and no one wanted to dispute it. The tribes accepted Alexander as their king and furnished him with gold and silver and supplies for his army, as well as soldiers and chariots to become part of the army. There was occasional resistance, and sometimes a revolt would flare up in a region Alexander had passed through, but these were always speedily defeated. When the army reached the sea, some seven months after it had started out, southern India was a conquered land.

A Deadly March and a Reunion

The "sea" that Alexander's fleet and army had reached was actually what today is called the Gulf of Oman. It is part of the Indian Ocean that lies between the nations of Oman and Iran, which in Alexander's time was part of the Persian Empire. By crossing the Indus and marching west, the army would eventually reach the Persian province of Carmania. However, to get there, it would have to pass through an unknown region.

Alexander decided to start the army out first and have the fleet follow it along the coastline two months later. The ships were warships and could not carry much water or stores of food, so the army would have to dig wells and leave piles of supplies all along the coast for the crews.

The army set out in late August of 325 B.C., with wagons full of flour, dried meat, and containers of water. It probably numbered eighty thousand foot soldiers, eighteen thousand cavalry, and an unknown number of women and children, scientists and seers, and others. The fleet was ordered to sail in October.

Everything went well for a time. But then the army reached a stretch of coastline that was dry, sandy desert. Marching became difficult and water became precious. The suffering from heat and thirst became severe, especially among the women and children who were with the army. It was said that many thousands of them died. Once again, Alexander tried to be an example. He marched on foot as his men were doing, and went without water as they did.

Finally, the army reached the Persian province of Gedrosia, where water and food were plentiful. From there, the army went on to the province of Carmania. In Carmania, in January of 324 B.C., Alexander was approached by a group of ragged, longhaired, shaggy-bearded men who turned out to be Alexander's loyal admiral Nearchus and some of his officers. They and their crews had been on the open sea under a scorching sun for several months, only going ashore to pick up the supplies Alexander had left along the coast. They seemed to be in such bad shape that Alexander cried out, "What happened to the fleet? Are you all that is left?"[3]

Nearchus quickly assured Alexander that most of the ships and crewmen had reached a safe harbor after a long, difficult journey. In making the voyage, Nearchus had become the first man to chart the coast, rocks, shallows, and islands of the Gulf of Oman. This would be of tremendous use to future sailors, and it had largely been Alexander's idea to do it.

Alexander Returns to Persia

It was not until the spring of 324 B.C. that the army finally marched into the Persian city of Susa. Alexander found there had been widespread wrongdoing while he had been gone. Some of the men he had appointed governors of provinces had acted badly. They had robbed and looted their provinces of their treasure, created unjust laws, and destroyed much of the good Alexander had done. Alexander handed out harsh punishments and made new appointments. Soon, things were back in order in the city.

It began to seem that Alexander planned to unite all the lands he ruled in Asia with Macedonia, Greece, and Thrace as one grand nation. It was said that he hoped to bring people from Asia to Europe and from Europe to Asia, and unite them by marriage until the two continents became much like each other. Perhaps this was why in the spring of 324 B.C. he oversaw the marriage of ten thousand of his Macedonian and Greek soldiers to women they had paired up with from various parts of the Persian Empire, giving them all gifts of money. He himself also married two more wives from different parts of the empire. One was Statira, the daughter of Darius, who became regarded as Alexander's queen, over Roxana. Almost nothing is known of any of Alexander's wives, but it seems clear that Roxana must have hated Statira, for she eventually murdered her by poisoning!

All this attention that Alexander seemed to be paying to Persians caused resentment among his veteran Macedonian troops. They became afraid that he intended to make Persia, rather than Macedonia, the center of the empire. There was a near mutiny, with Alexander and his soldiers shouting at each other. Finally, Alexander was able to convince them that he did not intend to do any of the things about which they were concerned.

In the late summer, Alexander's great friend, Hephaestion, became ill and died. This was a terrible blow to Alexander. He was grief stricken for days, and some say he never recovered.

THE DEATH OF A GOD

In late winter of 324 B.C., Alexander sent a strange letter to all the cities of the Greek league. He announced that he wished to be worshipped throughout Greece as a god!

Did Alexander actually think he was a god? Some historians have thought so. Others have not. In Alexander's time, people believed that instead of blood, gods had a magical liquid called ichor flowing in their bodies. Once, when Alexander was wounded and blood was flowing from the wound, he pointed at it and said, "This, you see, is blood, and not such ichor as flows from wounds of the immortals."[4] It seems clear that he was trying to show everyone around him that he was *not* a god. The announcement that he was a god was probably what we would now call a political move, which he felt would make it easier for him to rule such a vast empire. At any rate, the Greek city-states agreed to follow his request and honor him as a god.

As 323 B.C. began, Alexander was planning for an invasion of Arabia in the summer. He apparently intended to then continue on along the North African coast, capture the Phoenician city of Carthage, then cross the Mediterranean Sea and conquer Spain. Some historians believe that this shows that Alexander actually intended to try to conquer the entire world of his time and create a worldwide empire. Others disagree. They think that if Alexander had wanted to conquer his whole world, he would have kept on going farther into India when he had the chance.

Whatever Alexander's plans were, they were interrupted. In early June he came down with a fever. As days went by, his condition grew worse, and he took to his bed. By the tenth day, it was clear to everyone that he was dying. His Macedonian soldiers came to pass by his bed, one after another, and he could only smile at them. It was said that when one of Alexander's generals bent over him and asked who he was leaving his kingdom to, Alexander replied in a weak whisper, "To the best man."[5] He died on June 10, 323 B.C., at the age of thirty-two. For many centuries, some historians believed that Alexander had been poisoned by someone who hoped to take his

WHAT HAPPENED TO ALEXANDER'S EMPIRE?

Some time after Alexander's death, his wife Roxana had a baby boy, the heir to Alexander's empire. However, soon after his birth, both he and Roxana were murdered, probably by one of Alexander's generals. Following Alexander's death, his generals began seizing control of parts of the empire. They made themselves kings and began fighting with one another, trying to gain full control of the empire. These wars went on for forty years, and succeeded only in breaking up the empire.

place. But today, from the description of Alexander's symptoms, most doctors believe he died from the disease malaria.

Alexander's body was embalmed, and it lay in state in Babylon for two years. Then it was decided it should be sent back to Macedonia and entombed there. However, before this could be done, Alexander's friend Ptolemy seized control of the body and took it to Egypt, which he now ruled. There, he had the body entombed in the city of Memphis. Later he had it moved to Alexandria. For hundreds of years the tomb was visited by Roman emperors. Gradually, it was covered up. Today, no one knows exactly where it is.

WHY ALEXANDER WAS CALLED "GREAT"

King Alexander of Macedonia was the first person in history to be called "the Great."[6] He was given this title some years after his death, mainly due to his victories

After Alexander's death, one of his generals, Lysimachus, was given control of Thrace. Lysimachus had coins made with Alexander's image. A ram's horn on Alexander's head identified him with the Egyptian god Ammon, the sun god.

and conquests. He certainly *was* a successful conqueror; his armies marched more than twenty thousand miles, gaining control over Illyria, Thrace, Greece, Asia Minor, and western and southern India. And it seems clear that he intended to continue conquering, for he was planning an invasion of Arabia when he became ill and died.

Alexander was first and foremost a soldier. It is obvious that he really enjoyed fighting battles and engaging in hand-to-hand combat. As a general, he was able to notice an opponent's mistake in a flash, and take instant advantage of it. He could improvise brilliant new uses of weapons and strategies that caught his enemies by surprise and shattered their plans.

He was a great leader, never asking his soldiers to do anything that he himself would not do or did not do. He was an example to them, whether wading through mountain snow in bone-chilling cold or trudging over a sandy desert in hammering heat with a desperate thirst. He looked after them in every way possible. They loved

Alexander the Great had a grand funeral procession.

him for his treatment of them, his skill as a general, and his courage.

A Man Who Changed His World

There is no doubt that Alexander was responsible for the deaths of many thousands of people, who all might have gone on living if he had not insisted on conquering their lands. He was also responsible for having many thousands of conquered people turned into slaves for the rest of their lives. He caused the destruction of a number of cities, turning them into burned-out ruins.

He was hated by many of the people he conquered. To this day, in parts of the nation of Iran, which was the heart of ancient Persia, he is known as "Alexander the Accursed!" If a young Iranian child misbehaves, the mother will warn that Alexander will come and get him or her! He is thought of as a monster.[7]

Alexander was willing to take cold-blooded actions that he felt were for the good of his empire and army, such as the execution of his loyal old general Parmenio.

He apparently had a quick, vicious temper that led him to do terrible things, such as the murder of his friend Cleitus.

However, Alexander also did some admirable things. By taking scientists along with his army, he did much to add to Greek science and knowledge. He actually built far more cities than he destroyed. He seems to have had a great plan of uniting all his conquests into a vast empire, made up of many nationalities of people, living and working together in peace. He is given credit as the person who set the stage for what has become known as the Hellenistic Age—the period of history when Greek art, philosophy, and science were spread throughout the heart of the western world. This was an extremely important era in world history.

Over the centuries, many historians felt that Alexander was basically just a ruthless, bloodthirsty warrior who actually intended to try to conquer the entire world. Others have believed he was a man with a great dream of trying to create an empire that would be a "brotherhood" of all people. Whichever he was, the things Alexander did changed his world completely, in ways that still affect us today. Only a most unusual and brilliant person could have had the effect on the world that Alexander did.

CHRONOLOGY

356 B.C.—*July*: Alexander is born.

342 B.C.—*July*: Alexander enters the School of Pages. Aristotle is hired to become Alexander's teacher.

340 B.C.—Philip makes Alexander regent of Macedonia. Alexander fights his first battle and defeats the rebellious Maedi people.

338 B.C.—*August 2*: The Battle of Chaeronea.

336 B.C.—*October*: Alexander becomes king of Macedonia.

335 B.C.—*Spring to September*: Alexander campaigns against the Triballi in Thrace and the Dardanians and Taulantians in Illyria.
October: Thebes is destroyed. The Greek League agrees to name Alexander Captain-General of Macedonian and Greek forces for the war against Persia.

334 B.C.—*May*: Alexander lands in Asia, at Troy.
May–June: Alexander defeats a Persian force in the Battle of the Granicus.
Summer: Alexander captures Miletus and defeats the Persians at Halicarnassus.

333 B.C.—*April–July*: Alexander unties the Gordian knot.
November: Alexander defeats Darius at the Battle of Issus.

332 B.C.—*January–July*: Alexander conducts a seven-month siege of Tyre and captures it.

September–November: Alexander besieges Gaza and takes it.

December: Alexander and his army enter Egypt.

331 B.C.—*January*: Alexander founds the city of Alexandria.

February: Alexander visits the temple of Ammon at the oasis of Siwa.

October 1: Alexander defeats Darius at the Battle of Gaugamela, virtually destroying the Persian Empire.

330 B.C.—*January 30*: The Macedonian-Greek army enters the Persian capital, Persepolis, after defeating a Persian force protecting it.

May: The great palace of the Persian emperors in Persepolis is burned to the ground. Alexander takes the army out of Persepolis to search for Darius.

July: Darius is found murdered.

October: A plot to assassinate Alexander is discovered. Philotas and his father, Parmenio, are executed.

329 B.C.—*Spring*: Alexander crosses the mountains into the province of Bactria in search of Darius's murderers, who are led by the Persian noble Bessus. Bessus flees, crossing the Oxus River into the province of Sogdiana.

Summer: Alexander crosses the Oxus. Bessus is captured. The Scythians are encountered.

Autumn: Persian nobles lead a revolt against Alexander's occupation of Bactria and Sogdiana, and capture a number of Alexander's bases. He acts quickly to recapture them, and then decides he must prevent the Scythians from coming to help the rebels. He takes the army across the Jaxartes and defeats the Scythians in a battle. They promise not to assist the rebels.

328 B.C.—*Spring–Summer*: Alexander splits his army into small forces to chase down the rebels.

Autumn: Alexander murders Cleitus in Samarkand.

Winter: Alexander captures the rebel strongholds, the Sogdian Rock and Rock of Chorienes, and ends the revolt. He meets Roxana.

327 B.C.—*Spring*: A plot by some pages to murder Alexander is discovered.

326 B.C.—*Winter*: The invasion of India begins.

Spring: The army crosses the Indus River into India.

May: Alexander defeats Porus in the Battle of the Hydaspes River.

Summer: Alexander takes the army to the Hyphasis River. The soldiers mutiny and refuse to march any farther into India. Alexander gives in and agrees to return to Persia.

November: The army and fleet start down the Hydaspes River toward the coast.

325 B.C.—*Winter*: When two of the tribes threaten the movement of Alexander's army and fleet, he begins a campaign against them. He is badly wounded in an assault on a city, but the tribes finally give up.

August: Alexander and the army leave India and march toward Persia.

October: Nearchus and the fleet begin sailing along the Persian coast.

December: Alexander and the army re-enter Persia in the province of Carmania.

324 B.C.—*January*: Alexander and Nearchus meet in Carmania and Alexander learns that the fleet is safe.

February: Alexander and the army reach Susa.

Spring: Alexander arranges the marriage of ten thousand of his soldiers to Persian women and he himself marries two Persian women.

Summer: Hephaestion, Alexander's best friend, dies.

Autumn: Alexander sends a letter to the Greek League demanding to be worshipped as a god throughout Greece.

323 B.C.—*April*: Alexander goes to Babylon.

May: Alexander finishes preparations for an invasion of Arabia. He becomes ill.

June 10: Alexander dies.

CHAPTER NOTES

CHAPTER 1. KING, GENERAL, LEGEND

1. Robin Lane Fox, *The Search for Alexander* (Boston: Little, Brown and Company, 1980), p. 49.

2. Major General J. C. Fuller, *The Generalship of Alexander the Great* (New Brunswick, N.J.: Rutgers University Press, 1960), p. 263.

3. Plutarch, Moralia, in Will Durant, *The Life of Greece* (New York: Simon and Schuster, 1939), p. 539.

CHAPTER 2. WARFARE IN ALEXANDER'S TIME

1. Peter Connolly, *Greece and Rome at War* (Englewood Cliffs, N.J.: Prentice-Hall Inc., 1981), p. 40.

2. Theodore Ayrault Dodge, *Alexander* (New York: Da Capo Press, 1996), p. 140.

3. Connolly, p. 49.

4. Ibid.

5. Colonel Trevor N. Dupuy, U. S. A., Ret., *The Harper Encyclopedia of Military History* (New York: Harper Collins Publishers, 1993), p. 51.

6. Fletcher Pratt, *The Battles That Changed History* (Garden City, N.Y.: Hanover House, 1956), p. 26.

7. N. G. L. Hammond, *Alexander the Great: King, Commander, and Statesman* (Park Ridge, N.J.: Noyes Press, 1980), p. 19.

CHAPTER 3. ALEXANDER'S BOYHOOD

1. John V. A. Fine, *The Ancient Greeks: A Critical History* (Cambridge, Mass., and London: The Belknap Press of Harvard University, 1983), p. 627.

2. Demosthenes, *First Philippic*, in Ibid., p. 630.

3. Charles Mercer and the Editors of Horizon Magazine, *Alexander the Great* (New York: American Heritage Publishing Co., Inc., 1962), p. 16.

4. Plutarch, in Theodore Ayrault Dodge, *Alexander* (New York: Da Capo Press, 1996), p. 183.

5. N. G. L. Hammond, *The Genius of Alexander the Great* (Chapel Hill, N.C.: The University of North Carolina Press, 1997), p. 2.

6. Will Durant, *The Life of Greece* (New York: Simon and Schuster, 1939), p. 352.

7. Ibid., p. 538.

8. Plutarch, in Major General J. C. Fuller, *The Generalship of Alexander the Great* (New Brunswick, N.J.: Rutgers University Press, 1960), p. 57.

CHAPTER 4. ALEXANDER BECOMES KING

1. Theodore Ayrault Dodge, *Alexander* (New York: Da Capo Press, 1996), p. 128.

2. David J. Lonsdale, *Alexander the Great, Killer of Men* (New York: Carroll & Graff Publishers, 2004), p. 51.

3. N. G. L. Hammond, *Alexander the Great: King, Commander, and Statesman* (Park Ridge, N.J.: Noyes Press, 1980), p. 22.

4. Peter Green, *Alexander of Macedon, 356–323 B.C.: A Historical Biography* (Berkeley, Calif., and Los Angeles: University of California Press, 1991), p. 89.

5. Hammond, p. 36.

6. Ibid., p. 39.

CHAPTER 5. BATTLING BARBARIANS

1. Major General J. C. Fuller, *The Generalship of Alexander the Great* (New Brunswick, N.J.: Rutgers University Press, 1960), p. 83.

2. Arrian, *Anabasis of Alexander, Volume 1* (Cambridge, Mass.: Harvard University Press, 1929), p. 9.

3. Ibid., p. 13.

4. Ibid.

5. Fuller, p. 223.

CHAPTER 6. A VICTORY, A CITY'S DEMISE

1. Peter Green, *Alexander of Macedon, 356–323 B.C.: A Historical Biography* (Berkeley, Calif., and Los Angeles: University of California Press, 1991), p. 133.

2. Theodore Ayrault Dodge, *Alexander* (New York: Da Capo Press, 1996), p. 206.

3. Quintus Curtius Rufus, *The History of Alexander* (London: Penguin Books, 1984), p. 21.

4. Charles Mercer and the Editors of Horizon Magazine, *Alexander the Great* (New York: American Heritage Publishing Co., Inc., 1962), p. 47.

CHAPTER 7. INVASION OF AN EMPIRE

1. N. G. L. Hammond, *The Genius of Alexander the Great* (Chapel Hill, N.C.: The University of North Carolina Press, 1997), p. 64.

2. Ibid., p. 66.

3. Ibid., p. 68.

4. Ibid.

CHAPTER 8. BESIEGING PERSIA

1. N. G. L. Hammond, *The Genius of Alexander the Great* (Chapel Hill, N.C.: The University of North Carolina Press, 1997), p. 74.

2. Quintus Curtius Rufus, *The History of Alexander* (London: Penguin Books, 1984), p. 27.

3. Theodore Ayrault Dodge, *Alexander* (New York: Da Capo Press, 1996), p. 307.

4. Ibid., p. 309.

5. Arrian, *Anabasis of Alexander, Volume 1* (Cambridge, Mass.: Harvard University Press, 1929), p. 153.

6. N. G. L. Hammond, *Alexander the Great: King, Commander, and Statesman* (Park Ridge, N.J.: Noyes Press, 1980), p. 114.

7. Dodge, p. 340.

CHAPTER 9. KING OF EGYPT

1. Major General J. C. Fuller, *The Generalship of Alexander the Great* (New Brunswick, N.J.: Rutgers University Press, 1960), p. 216.

2. N. G. L. Hammond, *The Genius of Alexander the Great* (Chapel Hill, N.C.: The University of North Carolina Press, 1997), p. 102.

3. Quintus Curtius Rufus, *The History of Alexander* (London: Penguin Books, 1984), p. 78.

4. Theodore Ayrault Dodge, *Alexander* (New York: Da Capo Press, 1996), p. 363.

5. Robin Lane Fox, *The Search for Alexander* (Boston: Little, Brown and Company, 1980), p. 216.

6. Fuller, p. 164.

CHAPTER 10. AN EMPEROR'S END

1. Charles Mercer and the Editors of Horizon Magazine, *Alexander the Great* (New York: American Heritage Publishing Co., Inc., 1962), p. 102.

2. Michael Wood, *In the Footsteps of Alexander the Great* (Berkeley, Calif., and Los Angeles: University of California Press, 1997), p. 114.

3. Theodore Ayrault Dodge, *Alexander* (New York: Da Capo Press, 1996), p. 425.

CHAPTER 11. PURSUING THE ENEMY

1. Michael Wood, *In the Footsteps of Alexander the Great* (Berkeley, Calif., and Los Angeles: University of California Press, 1997), p. 134.

2. Charles Mercer and the Editors of Horizon Magazine, *Alexander the Great* (New York: American Heritage Publishing Co., Inc., 1962), p. 121.

3. Plutarch, Moralia, in N. G. L. Hammond, *Alexander the Great: King, Commander, and Statesman* (Park Ridge, N.J.: Noyes Press, 1980), p. 261.

CHAPTER 12. THE SCYTHIANS AND BEYOND

1. Theodore Ayrault Dodge, *Alexander* (New York: Da Capo Press, 1996), p. 474.

2. Ibid., p. 475.

3. Michael Wood, *In the Footsteps of Alexander the Great* (Berkeley, Calif., and Los Angeles: University of California Press, 1997), p. 162.

4. Dodge, p. 502.

CHAPTER 13. INVADING INDIA

1. Peter Green, *Alexander of Macedon, 356–323 B.C.: A Historical Biography* (Berkeley, Calif., and Los Angeles: University of California Press, 1991), p. 381.

2. Major General J. C. Fuller, *The Generalship of Alexander the Great* (New Brunswick, N.J.: Rutgers University Press, 1960), p. 57.

3. Arrian, *Anabasis of Alexander, Volume 2* (Cambridge, Mass.: Harvard University Press, 1933), p. 47.

4. Diodorus, in Theodore Ayrault Dodge, Alexander (New York: Da Capo Press, 1996), p. 562.

CHAPTER 14. THE DEATH OF A GOD

1. Arrian, *Anabasis of Alexander, Volume 2* (Cambridge, Mass.: Harvard University Press, 1933), p. 93.

2. Ibid., p. 97.

3. Michael Wood, *In the Footsteps of Alexander the Great* (Berkeley, Calif., and Los Angeles: University of California Press, 1997), p. 216.

4. Plutarch, Moralia, in Will Durant, *The Life of Greece* (New York: Simon and Schuster, 1939), p. 549.

5. Quintus Curtius Rufus, *The History of Alexander* (London: Penguin Books, 1984), p. 245.

6. Peter Bamm, *Alexander the Great: Power as Destiny* (New York: McGraw-Hill Book Company, 1968), p. 307.

7. Wood, p. 117.

GLOSSARY

ARCHAEOLOGISTS—Scientists who study remains of past human cultures and historical events.

BARRAGE—The shooting of a large number of missiles that form a barrier to protect advancing or retreating troops.

COALITION—An alliance of a number of countries, political parties, etc., in order to achieve a certain result.

COURTIERS—The people who make up the court, or household, of a king.

DESECRATED—Treated shamefully or dishonorably.

EMISSARIES—Messengers sent to offer a deal, to agree to a demand, to surrender, to make peace, etc.

ORACLE—A person, generally a priest or priestess, who is believed to be able to speak for a god or goddess.

REGENT—A person specially selected to rule when the actual ruler is unable to, due to age, absence, disability, etc.

RITUALS—Special ceremonies believed to gain assistance from a god or spirit, or have a magical effect.

SACRILEGE—Disrespect toward a religion or religious place.

SENTRIES—Soldiers placed around encampments or fortresses to keep watch for enemy troops.

FURTHER READING

BOOKS

Bankston, John. *The Life and Times of Alexander the Great*. Hockessin, Del.: Mitchell Lane Publishers, 2005.

Greenblatt, Miriam. *Alexander the Great and Ancient Greece*. New York: Benchmark Books, 2000.

Nardo, Don. *Ancient Persia*. San Diego: Blackbirch Press, 2004.

INTERNET ADDRESSES

"Alexander the Great," *Macedonia.org.* © 1996–2000. <http://faq.macedonia.org/history/alexander.the.great.html> (September 26, 2005).

Ancient Macedonia. © 2004. <http://www.ancientmacedonia.com/> (September 26, 2005).

Knox, E.L. Skip. "Alexander the Great." *Boise State University: History of Western Civilization*. n.d. <http://history.boisestate.edu/westciv/alexander/> (September 26, 2005).

Index